THE ART OF
RACHEL WHITEREAD

 Thames & Hudson

THE ART OF
RACHEL WHITEREAD

edited by Chris Townsend

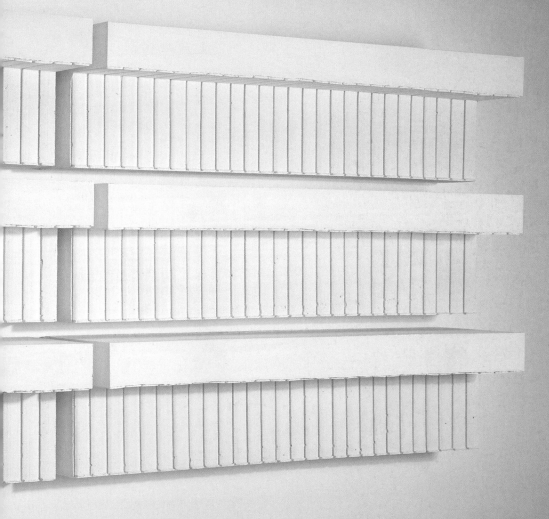

with 54 illustrations,
50 in color

CONTENTS

Cover
Monument (2001), resin and granite,
900 x 510 x 240cm (354 x 201 x 95in)
© Rachel Whiteread

Frontispiece
1 *Untitled (Collected Works)* 1998, plaster,
polystyrene and steel, 116 x 284 x 30cm
(45⅝ x 111¾ x 11¾in)

First published in 2004 in paperback in the
United States of America by Thames & Hudson Inc.,
500 Fifth Avenue, New York, New York 10110

thamesandhudsonusa.com

Library of Congress Catalog Card Number
2004100748

ISBN 0-500-28504-7

Printed and bound in Singapore

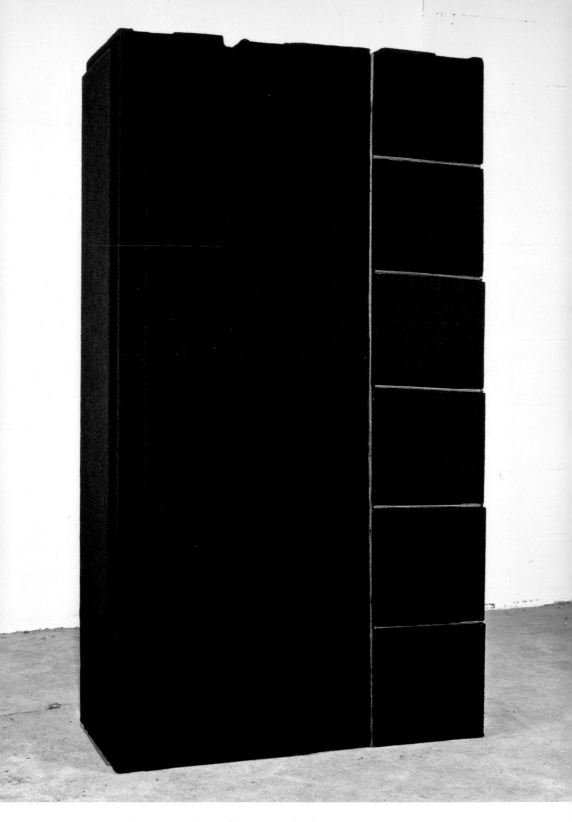

2   *Closet* 1988, plaster, felt and wood, 160 x 88 x 37cm (63 x 34⁵/₈ x 14⁵/₈in)

WHEN WE COLLIDE

History and Aesthetics, Space and Signs
in the Art of Rachel Whiteread

CHRIS TOWNSEND

'The great obsession of the nineteenth century was, as we know, history. (...) The present epoch will perhaps be above all the epoch of space.'

Michel Foucault, 'Of Other Spaces'

'I could tell you how many steps make up the streets rising like stairways, and the degree of the arcades' curves, and what kind of zinc scales cover the roofs; but I already know this would be the same as telling you nothing. The city does not consist of this, but of relationships between the measurements of space and the events of its past...'

Italo Calvino, Invisible Cities

I do not mean to be offensive when I say of Rachel Whiteread's early works that they are typically 'student' in their subject matter. The traces of mattresses (3, 9), wardrobes and baths (those revenants of the intimate and the domestic) *are* typical – not of student artworks, but of student spaces. They are, in the memory they quicken of stained, slack, fabric and scarred, calcified tubs, of splintered, lop-legged tables, of dusty vacuities beneath third-hand beds, of sun and water-stained paperbacks on windowsills, emblematic of a life in bed-sitters, in overcrowded, shared houses. This is, of course, not just the space of the student, but rather a condition of the city, of marginal spaces and temporary encounters that are, geographically, often central, but which exist economically and socially in what urban planners in more poetic times described as 'a twilight zone'. There is always furniture, too far gone for further use, propped against the brickwork at the sides of houses. Those Victorian residences, sub-subdivided into cubicles, their windows curtained with sheets or boards (or the cardboard boxes from the books you have just unpacked) are the homes of a twilight class – the poorly paid, the just-arrived, the not-quite-legally here, the couples crammed into mould stained rooms with sofa beds.

So Whiteread was, perhaps, engaged with the familiar objects of her recent past, as first undergraduate and then masters student. But there was about those objects nothing specific; even in their corporeal reference nothing that spoke of the significance of individual experience; about them nothing that sought to validate the particularity of the student-artist's life even as they resonated with the space and condition of the transient city dweller. Rather, in their very anonymity, those early objects articulated a shared experience rarely voiced by its subjects. But the process of abstraction, the solidifying of space into presence, meant that Whiteread could dwell upon those subjects – up to and including the most frequently footnoted topic of mortality – without the pathos that we might discern in Sickert, for example.

As Jennifer Gross notes, there is something of Chardin's cool scrutiny of the everyday in this. Regardless of the issue of mortality, we might see painting, and in particular the tradition of the *vanitas*, as Whiteread's inspiration, rather than sculpture – largely because of that tradition's concern with the everyday and the intimation of the unseen within its forms and reflections. Unlike the *vanitas* painters, Whiteread has no particular moral project: she does not employ a set of symbolic associations, rather she places the vernacular and the marginal at the centre of our attention. However, there may be, by virtue of undertaking such a project, a profound and necessary contingency between Whiteread's work and historical circumstance. Repeatedly the work asks of us, 'how do we live in this world, in this particular space?' As Shelley Hornstein points out, the considered placement of site specificity and the corresponding sense of dislocation that is manifest in all Whiteread's pieces, creates in us a sense of unfamiliarity. (What Hornstein, following the Russian theorist Victor Shklovsky, calls *ostraneniye* or making strange.) Those questions of how we live are asked through this alienation: as Hornstein puts it, the works 'exist to make us feel a sensation of life.'

3   *Untitled (Black Bed)* 1991, fibreglass and rubber, 30.5 x 188 x 137.2cm (12 x 74 x 54in)

There is, too, much that is 'conceptual' about Whiteread's work: as Susan Lawson remarks, turning to Marcel Duchamp's concept of *infra mince* as a theoretical means of apprehending the pellicle between absence and presence that seems to characterize pieces such as *Untitled (Wall)*, 1999 and *Ghost*, 1990. To this we might add something of the notion of the readymade: first as quotidian object, secondly as an object out of place, displaced here between negative and positive, then between the domestic space and the institution. Those voids of beds and baths were the not-very-special traces of not-very-special objects, made special. And to that add Duchamp's idea of an *art sec*, an art presented without affect or motivation; the object presented on its own terms.[1] It was this 'dryness' I think that enabled Whiteread to bypass the sentimentality that informs so many representations of the marginal. If those early pieces were bed-sitter objects rather than bed-sitter images, what they evoked about the conditions of life was that 'this is the way things are'.

Even if, as Lisa Dennison has observed, the nuances of surface in the casting in Whiteread's early works meant they 'lent themselves to the type of narrative interpretation that artists of previous generations had worked so carefully to avert'[2], the accompanying refusal of affect took Whiteread beyond the search for pity, either for the individual or the multitude who scurry anonymous between bed-sit, bus queue and stultifying job. Instead, she offered an uninflected vision of lives that are barely visible to other city dwellers – even to those who share the same spaces. Whiteread did this, most obviously, by making tangible that which wasn't there, by rendering visible the immaterial: but those materializations seemed to speak not of the personal, but of a collective, lived, historical experience. Gaston Bachelard cites the Lithuanian writer Oscar Vladislas de Lubicz Milosz (Oskarus Milasius) to the effect that 'A wardrobe is filled with the mute tumult of memories.'[3] What's fundamental to Whiteread's practice is the emphasis she places on the degree to which that tumult is shared, and the degree to which it is passed, like the item of furniture as hand-me-down, from one generation to another.

One of the first pieces to make obvious this emphasis on the communal was, at the same time, one that most blatantly manifested its art-historical lineage. As Melanie Mariño points out here, *Untitled (One Hundred Spaces)*, 1995 (8), made a

4   *Untitled* 1987, sellotape and air

5 *Untitled (Six Spaces)* 1994, resin, 6 units, size according to installation

6   *Untitled (25 Spaces)* 1995, resin, 25 units, size according to installation

specific reference to Bruce Nauman's *A Cast of the Space Under My Chair*, 1965–68. This was a work that Whiteread could have seen displayed in Nauman's 1988 exhibition at Whitechapel Art Gallery, by which time she was already making her own interior casts of domestic objects. These had included *Closet*, 1988 (2), taken from a wardrobe, and a 'cast' of a side table, wrapped in sellotape and then cut from it (4), made in 1987. That Whiteread chose to take on Nauman's piece suggests not that this was where her practice began, but that she felt there was more to be done with such a concept than Nauman had achieved. Certainly Whiteread seemed to recast minimalism, and those debates about where and what space was, and wasn't, that dominated post-minimal American art of the late 1960s and early '70s. The work returned us to Carl Andre's dictum – at least as defined on his behalf by Robert Smithson – that 'a thing is a hole in a thing it is not.'[4] But as Mariño observes nothing could have been more anathematic to minimalism than the metaphors for the body that cropped up throughout Whiteread's oeuvre. Where Nauman the post-minimalist was content to solidify the space under *his* chair, Whiteread multiplied it first by six (5), then by twenty-five (6), and eventually into a hundred variously coloured and sized resin casts, arrayed in the archetypal minimalist form of the grid, giving the piece a resonance with Sol LeWitt's *Serial Project* maquettes, 1966.

Such a strategy, from a young British artist, solicited immediate reference to Anthony Gormley's installation *Field for the British Isles*, 1993. In Gormley's work small, apparently identical, clay figures filled a room of Tate Liverpool, crowded together in an amorphous mass, their density denying the spectator access to the space, their 'eyes', pressed in the clay, alternately imploring and aggressive. It was only with time, relegated to the margins of this mob, that the spectator perceived differences between each hand-crafted statuette. *Field* offered a model of democracy and variant subjectivity – if you cared to look – in an era of insistent conformity. The same might be said of Whiteread's introduction of variability within the structural matrix of the grid. (It was, if you like, field without figure.) To a critic of the same generation as Whiteread, who had spent his childhood perched on hard wooden seats in sixties and seventies schoolrooms, it was tempting to interpret those 100

7 *Untitled (Floor)* 1994–95, resin, 25.4 x 274 x 396cm (10 x 108 x 156in)

8 *Untitled (One Hundred Spaces)* 1995, 100 units, size according to installation

anti-chairs as laid out in the pattern of a classroom. *Untitled (One Hundred Spaces)* was about the spaces under chairs, but here they were *ours*. The work was not simply an extension of Nauman's rather narcissistic conceit: rather it was about the differences between us, as individuals, and the way we still made up a community; and it was, in a sense, about our histories, about what had happened to us and our absented bodies since we sat in those chairs and paid attention to teacher.

If *Untitled (One Hundred Spaces)* was a piece that, in its unstable movement between abstraction and representation, proffered narratives of time and social relation within the confines of an unseen room, through the formal relationships of rectangular solids, Whiteread's earlier project *Ghost* had literalized a room to emphasize the closely packed connections of history it might contain. Where the one seemed to extend, the other compressed; and what Whiteread unpacked from within it was a fresh perspective on the histories space contained. Bachelard remarks that 'In its countless alveoli space contains compressed time. That is what space is for.'[5] In her solidification and inversion of spatial relations we can see Whiteread as bent on liberating that time and revealing its contents.

Mariño sees contingencies here with the work, grounded in the reinterpretation and reclamation of space, of members of the Anarchitecture group in the early 1970s. What *Ghost* seemed to have in common with those projects was a shared desire to break through what Gordon Matta-Clark, Anarchitecture's most prominent figure, described as 'hard-shelled cultural reality'. We might understand this as a 'political' project, exposing the metaphorical and literal constructs of ideology as it is materialized in buildings. *Ghost* seemed to work only at the level of the personal – as an invocation of the room's inhabitants whose traces had seeped into its walls and been dissipated in its atmosphere – and the formal. As Jennifer Gross notes, Whiteread seemed to be 'persevering under the conviction that form is the end to its own means for an artist and that this is an inherently lively enough endeavour that the viewer will be compelled into their own engaged...experience.' That conviction had last been most clearly stated in the early 1970s, where in addition to the members of Anarchitecture we find it in the work of Dennis Oppenheim, dealing with public institutions such as the New York Stock Exchange and Stedelijk

Museum, or Richard Serra, in the disturbance of the public sphere: work that in its compulsion articulated a particular concern with the ideology of space.

Whiteread's move from domestic fittings and spaces as subjects into the domain of public art would make obvious, and therefore contestable, the apparently natural (and therefore non-ideological) ideologies embedded in the structures she chose. *House*, 1992, was *just* the internal cast of a Victorian terraced property, 193 Grove Road, in Bow, east London; a scaling up of the formal concerns of *Ghost* in a building scheduled for demolition. That *just* doesn't explain why the work caused such a public furore, successfully alienating civic bureaucrats and finding for the artist a suite of unlikely allies. As Angela Dimitrakaki puts it, '*House* was relevant to a wider realm of intersecting debates ranging from the meaning of public space in art (and vice versa) to the meaning of democracy, with the relationship between the two being clearly the most unsettling of these exchanges.' Amongst the debates that *House* provoked were the question of ageing housing stock and what to do with it, the process of gentrification in formerly solid working class districts of the East End, and the question of who planned urban change. Even as it solidified as a terrifying manifestation of what Dimitrakaki refers to as 'the political unconscious', *House* was meant to be temporary: it was only planned to stand for three months. Demolishing the work in January 1994, Tower Hamlets Council, having most reason to fear it, couldn't get rid of the work fast enough, adopting much the same attitude as they took towards their older housing stock. The work's continuing effect, its permanence, is a consequence of its destruction.

But like most works of public art the project was necessarily embedded in the issues that it came to critique. *House* was not that wholly quiescent and unproblematic object beloved of public arts agencies – in which the spectator is temporarily arrested and amused, and the commissioning corporation or state agency allowed to claim that they have done their bit for culture. *House* was created as a project within 'urban renewal'. The situation was one of dislocation, one of those familiar scenarios where Victorian terraces give way to the down-sized, tissue-walled, new-housing of the civic authority; give way too, to parkland and ameliorative, redemptive, public art projects. *House* was created by an artist associated, by the press at least, with a movement (the YBAs) already implicated, however unknowingly, in the nascent gentrification of other parts of east London. For it remains a truism of metropolitan life that those unappealing areas where young artists find cheap studio space will sooner or later prove an irresistible lure to trendy merchant bankers (if that last term's not an oxymoron). Pamela Lee elucidates this process in the history of New York's SoHo, and the role of Whiteread's *Water Tower*, 1998, as perhaps unwitting commentary. As in Manhattan, so in London: or more specifically Clerkenwell, Hoxton, Shoreditch, and these days Hackney. *House* embodied conformity to a certain conception of public art – as sanctioned cultural placebo at a site of alienation. But *House* was also a wholly dissident intervention in the processes of dislocation around that site. It reformulated, for art-world and public institution alike, the formerly safe understanding of what 'public' art was meant to do for its public and how it was meant to do it. After *House*, public art in Britain could never be the same again: the work demonstrated that rather than merely placate audiences, art still had the capacity to provoke through its address to history.

  House, despite its antecedents in post-minimalism, was a profoundly humanistic work. It registered what it meant to be a human subject, across time, in an architectural space. Like *Untitled (One Hundred Spaces)* the work was charged with the human even as it emphasized anonymity. Probably that was why Councillor Eric Flounders of the local civic authority described *House* as an 'excrescence': to that breed of legislators and bureaucrats who like their populace anonymous, the more easily to move them around, the site was an irritation to be cleansed as soon as possible. The clerks who sanctioned the Artangel project – probably expecting something altogether neutered – might not have had the wit to articulate the discomfort it created for their residual consciences, but they knew enough to relate symptom to cause. Adrian Searle summed it up beautifully when he wrote:

> What, finally, has been exposed is an empty setting, a place where people once led a life of intimacies, grew up, grew old and died. And, one might add, fucked, rowed, worried, slept, ate, shat, fought, laughed and lied. No one looks out of the windows anymore, no one

puts out the milk-bottles on the stoop; no one shouts 'Kevin come in your tea's ready' or returns home late from the pub and fumbles with the keys to the lock.'[6]

The chilly ratiocinators of regulatory authorities don't like to be reminded too often or too hard that the subjects of their decisions are flesh and blood individuals with uneasy, unregulatable lives.

The furore created by *House* served to further link Whiteread to the YBAs. (For there were moments in the early 1990s when being an artist seemed to consist solely of being in the papers, rather than – notwithstanding the work of Sarah Lucas – turning their contents into art.) In retrospect, however, *House* allows us to isolate Whiteread's practice as unusual for a successful British artist of the last two decades. Whiteread – born 1963 – was of the same generation as the YBAs, but she was not a product of Goldsmiths or St. Martins, those schools that turned out many of the bright young things of the late eighties and early nineties. Whiteread had trained first at Brighton, as a painter, before turning to sculpture during her masters degree at the Slade School of Art. Few of her tutors could be described as having those conceptualist interests that characterized the teaching at the more fashionable London colleges. Whiteread did not participate in the 'Freeze' exhibition, which has come to define the starting point for the YBAs as a movement. Her work had already been included in the 'Whitworth's Young Contemporaries' exhibition in 1987, the 'Riverside Open' of 1988, and the 'Whitechapel Open' of 1989; all conventional elements in the institutional acceptance of young artists in Britain.

Furthermore, whilst Whiteread became part of the milieu that was so vital to the formation of the YBA ethos, her work had little in common with much that emerged from its studios. There was about Whiteread's output a sense of scrupulous meditation, of prior thought and accuracy of achievement, that contrasted to the more intuitive approach of some of her contemporaries. For many YBAs it didn't seem to matter if the work 'worked'; there would always be another piece to follow it. With Whiteread you got the sense that every piece she made mattered: an unusual attitude at a time when being an artist seemed something quite frivolous. That seriousness extended to the readings the work provoked: most YBAs

9   *Untitled (Air Bed II)* 1992, rubber and neoprene, 120 x 197 x 23cm (47^{1}/$_{4}$ x 77^{5}/$_{8}$ x 9in)

eschewed overt relationships between their work and history. Whiteread could not only do 'formal', she could do 'history' too, and consistently combine both in complex and provocative ways, whereas when other young artists did this, as Marcus Harvey did with *Myra*, 1995, it seemed to be more a matter of luck than judgement.

Within a month or so of being forced into public attention by the controversy surrounding *House*, Whiteread was back in the spotlight. This time it was as recipient of the Tate Gallery's Turner Prize for 1993. The Turner, which had been initiated largely as a long-service award to British artists for bloody-minded persistence in the face of near-universal indifference, had been reformulated once it became clear to the Tate's organizers that the media phenomenon that was Young British Art also provided them with ready opportunities for shameless self-publicity. (Though in their reports to their statutory funding agencies they doubtless dignified the media scrum and swelling numbers attending Turner Prize exhibitions under the shibboleth of 'increased accessibility'.) Whiteread was thus thrown into a situation where artists were perceived, and promoted, as part of the spectacle of current events and culture rather than as perceptive commentators on that spectacle *and* reflexively aware practitioners within it. The publicity generated by the revised format of the Turner added a great deal of heat to debates around contemporary art, but little light. Perhaps that there was a debate at all was enough for those bound up in the complex business of funding and running the country's premier art institution on a very frayed shoestring. Since few mass-media commentators other than Searle and Andrew Graham-Dixon could conceptualize Whiteread's work in terms more sophisticated than those that could be elicited in the course of a cab ride (for that seemed to be where they furnished their ideas, if not, for Brian Sewell, his sesquipedalian vocabulary) there was very little hope for a protracted and developing discussion around the formal and historical issues it raised.

House was a turning point in Whiteread's career: certainly the thickening of memory that was the nub of the work had already been explored in *Ghost* and the smaller domestic pieces, but now that theme was made publicly manifest. What was rendered visible was something that *had* once belonged, unrecognized, in the public domain. Whiteread demonstrated the capacity, latent in those early works, to refer from the singular experience of space (the bed-sitter baths and mattresses) to the communal, and significantly, to the communitarian. First with *House*, then *Water Tower*, then *Holocaust Memorial*, 2000, *Monument*, 2001, and most recently *Room 101*, 2003, Whiteread wrested anamnesis from amnesia. These, I would argue, were profoundly 'political' gestures, because each restored to public consciousness lives, and the memories of lives, that had been, or which were being, elided by the processes of historical transformation; memories which the dominant discourses that motivate such transformation often would have rather remained invisible. Michel Foucault, in formulating a theory of power structured around discourses – who is allowed to speak, where and with what effect they are allowed to speak – once remarked 'My object is not language but the archive, that is to say the accumulated existence of discourse.'[7] There are discourses within those relations of power which Foucault maps that were in the moment of their articulation subordinated, scarcely heard, or which, once significant, have faded to the point where they are no longer recognizable. This is the place in the archive, that space of accumulated discourse and its material effects, where Whiteread intervenes. It is, I suspect, no accident that at times in her career Whiteread has indeed literalized this gesture, tracing the antitheses of archives. (10)

As Pamela Lee observes in her essay on *Water Tower*, Whiteread's installation in downtown Manhattan, the work reflected the historical dislocations enacted over the last forty years in the streets beneath its roof-top location. In its self-reflexive formal properties *Water Tower* narrated a displacement from industrial site to anonymous sculpture: but at the same time it reflected upon a corresponding shift in land-use, where property value was transformed by the activity of artists. SoHo moved from being a decaying industrial site to become a region of artistic bohemia, then in the 1980s a heady and expensive blend of art galleries and high fashion, and finally, in the mid 1990s a high-rent, heritage-mall housing trendy but ubiquitous brands for out-of-town shoppers. Lee's essay offers a condensed history of site specific art and a site specific artwork that condenses history: an equivalent perhaps to the mirroring effect of *Water Tower* itself, seen at certain angles and times of day.

As a metaphor of circulation and mobility, *Water Tower* was a perfect sign for the instability of the city *sui generis* and of the specific space in which it was installed, only the flows it represented were as much those of capital and fashion as they were of water. Once again, the formal properties of one of Whiteread's public sculptures seemed to map the discourses that shaped the streets it overlooked.

In a footnote to his book *Archive Fever* that establishes a curious parallel with the thought of Foucault, Jacques Derrida remarks 'There is no political power without control of the archive, if not of memory. Effective democratization can always be measured by this essential criterion: the participation in and the access to the archive, its constitution, and its interpretation.'[8] This brief passage has an extraordinary resonance for Whiteread's practice as an artist, both in the presentation and reception of her work. Leaving aside the further resonance of the Greek *Arkhē* (commencement) and its derivative *arkheion* (shelter, house), Derrida's comment opens a set of concerns that are fundamental for Whiteread: the nature of memory, and vitally, 'politically', the question of who remembers and how, of who orders the social space of memory. We imagine space to be neutral: indeed, we imagine space to be empty. Whiteread's undertaking demonstrates again and again not only that space in its apparent emptiness is profoundly ideological and constructed, but that space comes with its own histories, and that what seems to be void is a plenitude. What's at the heart of this demonstration is the freshly embodied language of space. The gaps in the quotidian matrix of our lives 'speak'.

For Blake Stimson what is 'spoken' is an attempt to mediate subjectivity in an age of subjective oblivion. Rather than simply speaking memory, Whiteread moves between the condition of the self and the condition of the object. In this sense her work, even at its most concrete, 'shimmers'. On the one hand the alienation of subjectivity, its being bound by industrial forms, is embodied, literally, in the sign of her work. On the other, presence looms large, announces its identity. Looking at Whiteread's castings, one experiences oneself embedded in the inert. One has, as Whiteread remarks of herself, 'become the wall'. Stimson suggests there is a certain self-conscious rectitude to this, a stoic acceptance of one's alienation and one's irrelevance to history. (Especially a history where life is, effectively, conveyed by and lived within industrial forms.) We might add that this rectitude is, to a degree, reflected in the formal serenity of Whiteread's works. But the 'shimmer' of industrial form that Whiteread produces – that is the use of industrial processes to make emphatic signs of elided life – points not only to historical impotence, but suggests a condition of self-enlightenment about that condition.

This is, for Stimson, at least a gesture towards an apparently outmoded notion of subjectivity, a display of 'all the potential of self-identification, without ever getting there.' In itself this is a crucial intervention by an artist, for it is not a nostalgic glance towards a golden age of bourgeois identity, replete with self-comprehension and autonomy. Rather it has, as we shall see, much to say about the condition of the human subject in our world, as we live in it, here and now. Rather than just being 'historically reflective' Whiteread's work is also 'immediately relevant'. Stimson remarks that 'what was given up as the bourgeoisie abandoned its markers of self, its propriety, was the boundedness that made identity legible, that prevented it from folding into the market as just one more commodity form.' In the age of post-industrial capitalism, when 'human resources' have become its most important raw material, when identity and space have become commodity forms, Whiteread's insistence on a *boundary* of the self, whilst simultaneously embodying the kind of post-structuralist decentring of sign and subject pointed to by Susan Lawson, is an act of the utmost importance, even if its probity seems doomed.

James Young's essay on Whiteread's *Holocaust Memorial* in Vienna takes us to the artist's most direct, and perhaps most controversial, engagement with history. Young suggests that the most effective memorial to the catastrophe had to be one that refused closure, that denied the completion of memory, in the same moment as it recovered memory. As Young puts it, 'Can a void be articulated formally without seeming to fill it in with the formal object itself, its meanings and memory of an absence?' For Whiteread, of course, the absence of the object is the formal core of her work; but this does not mean that she signifies only absence, rather provokes reflection on the meanings of that absence. This reflection proved problematic for some Viennese. The *Judenplatz* site was a palimpsest of anti-Semitic actions, and the protests against Whiteread's planned intervention within the square were perhaps less to do with the potential loss of revenue by shopkeep-ers than with a looming presence that might remind Vienna's citizens of the his-torical tradition of Jewish persecution, and of Austria's complicity with Nazism.

Whiteread chose the library as her model for *Holocaust Memorial*, but it was a library you could never access. Previously, with pieces such as *Sequel IV*, 2002, and *Untitled (Book Corridors)*, 1997–98, she had cast the spaces around and behind books. *Holocaust Memorial* was an architecture of such books – a fit memorial to the people of the book; reminder of all the books burned by the fascists in the 1930s and '40s; and chilling reminder that bodies were burned as easily and remorse-lessly as paper. That, *Holocaust Memorial* seemed to suggest, was a historical loss beyond restitution, a memory that could not be regained. But if we could not, from our moment in history, understand what the catastrophe of the Holocaust meant to European culture in the terms of what *might* have happened, we could continually apprehend it in terms of what *did*. It seems appropriate that *Holocaust Memorial* lit-erally took the form of an archive. Young rightly remarks of Whiteread, Horst Hoheisel and other makers of Holocaust monuments that they refuse to domesti-cate memory; they do not allow redemption. This is because they refuse also to close the book: the Holocaust is not over; it resonates into our present moment and beyond. History is never over: an archive is by its nature open-ended, accretive. We never know completely what its contents are, what it means, or what it will come to mean. Perhaps those artists have grasped intuitively what Derrida theorizes:

> The question of the archive is not...a question of the past. It is not
> the question of a concept dealing with the past that might *already*
> be at our disposal or not at our disposal, *an archivable concept of the*
> *archive*. It is a question of the future, the question of the future
> itself, the question of a response, of a promise and of a responsi-
> bility for tomorrow. The archive: if we want to know what it will
> have meant, we will only know in times to come. Perhaps.[9]

Chris Townsend's essay on *Monument* takes Whiteread's response to the most prominent public space in Britain as exemplary of the artist's larger project. With *Monument* Whiteread again demonstrated that she could combine formal issues (in

26

10 *Untitled (Book Corridors)* 1997–98, plaster, polystyrene, steel and wood
overall dimensions 222 x 427 x 523cm (87^3/$_8$ x 168^1/$_8$ x 205^7/$_8$in)

Archive (+ Hol Memorial)

the way in which the work reprises and extends the modernist explorations of material and spectatorship undertaken by Boccioni, Gabo and Tatlin) with a profound awareness of the historical issues both embodied in the monuments that seemingly define Trafalgar Square and disembodied in the memories that surround them. Permeating this study is a Foucaultian critique of the manifestations of institutional power. As Thomas Flynn points out, Foucault's account of the displacement of the economy of power into the unseen is grounded in spatial terminology.[10] That history of displacement is, in part, one of a retreat from monumental expression as power no longer needs to be enforced by the autocratic state, but becomes invisible and permeating as the disciplining of the subject is carried out largely by the subject itself within the democratic society. Whiteread's response to Trafalgar Square is not simply to the 'disciplinary monuments' contained there as representatives of an autocratic, imperial history, however fissured. Rather, *Monument* can be understood as a critique of the disappearance of institutional power into what portrays itself as benevolent, ideology-free neutrality, and what is, in reality, a sophisticated form of organising subjectivity. As unstable archive, a vessel for England past, present and future, *Monument* mimed that condition of contemporary architecture, defined by Rem Koolhaas, in which 'Transparency only reveals everything in which you cannot partake.'[11]

Whiteread's responses to public space and collective memory suggest a further Foucaultian concept, that of the 'heterotopia'. Towards the end of his life Foucault defined that idea as dealing with 'those singular spaces to be found in some given social spaces whose functions are different or even the opposite of others.'[12] Certainly *House* (a home you can't live in) and *Water Tower* (a storage vessel that you can't keep water in) exemplify that reversal of function in public space, but *Monument* is not a plinth that can bear no sculpture. What the transparent *Monument* bears is beneath it: a visible, tangible plinth that cannot carry any visible, tangible manifestation of power, but which has become a temporary space for the installation of 'improving' art work. Whiteread makes a critique of space not through function but through what is manifested in space, with the installation of art itself a sign of a certain kind of power.

Whilst he returned to it in the 1980s Foucault's concept of the 'heterotopia' first surfaces in the mid 1960s, and, as Benjamin Genocchio has pointed out, in its various manifestations there is a flexibility of use and definition that is both confusing and potentially useful.[13] In the preface to *The Order of Things*, Foucault invokes the heterotopia as a place, contrasted to the utopia, which represents a disordering effect. To this point he has been concerned with Borges's wondrous taxonomy of animals from a 'certain Chinese encyclopaedia';[14] a reordering of the obvious which for Foucault 'shattered...all the familiar landmarks of my thought – *our* thought...breaking up all the ordered surfaces and all the planes on which we are accustomed to tame the wild profusion of existing things.'[15] Foucault then moves from textual ontologies to spatial ones:

> *Heterotopias* are disturbing, probably because they secretly under-mine language, because they make it impossible to name this *and* that, because they shatter or tangle common names, because they destroy 'syntax' in advance, and not only the syntax with which we construct sentences but also that less apparent syntax which causes words and things...to 'hold together'. (...) Heterotopias...desiccate speech, stop words in their tracks, contest the very possibility of grammar at its source.[16]

Although we should qualify it as a singular object where Foucault is imagin-ing heterotopic space as characterized by the assemblage of heterogeneous ele-ments, *Monument* is an example of this kind of activity in its blocking and invert-ing of the rules of monumental rhetoric. Indeed, the work appears to incorporate the hierarchical ordering of things within a different order so as to demonstrate the ideologically constructed nature of what seems wholly natural. But *Monument* was only a partial and temporary intervention in a utopian syntactical space (in that Trafalgar Square is an idealized model of state authority). So, for Townsend, here what's equally useful in understanding the historical commentary implicit in *Monument's* brief life as a site-specific sculpture is Foucault's looser conception of the heterotopia, outlined in a lecture given in 1967, but not published until 1984.[17] Such sites are characterized as much by networks of relation as they are by archi-tectural or geographic limits (7). (Foucault discusses the house, the bedroom, the bed; all spaces that have a massive significance within Whiteread's oeuvre.)[18]

29

I'd propose that the question of unknown or temporary relation is vital to all the objects Whiteread casts: these are objects we pass from one to another (like books or furniture); spaces where we pass one another. (How many people have slept, before us, in the beds we now occupy? How about the bedrooms?) We can see Trafalgar Square itself as, momentarily, becoming a heterotopia in its temporary slips from utopian site to one of disruption (in demonstrations and spontaneous celebrations by those largely excluded from the discourses of the utopian state, who meet as strangers in those moments and who leaving the space become strangers once again). It is this capacity of the single space to be something different, at different times, that was reflected in the shimmering transience of *Monument*.

I want to suggest, however, that this observation of the overlooked is not *simply* a humanist project that insists, as it certainly does, on the dignity of the ephemeral human subject. It is, perhaps, a mark of the truly significant artist that, however unknowingly, their work anticipates the shifts of the present that come to compose history, as much as it, without flinching, confronts and interprets the past. Whiteread's public art projects in particular, from *House* to *Room 101*, can be seen as fulfilling such an anticipatory function. This quality of being both 'in time' and 'ahead of time' might well explain those 'uncanny' characteristics so often ascribed to the artist's work.[19] (It also suggests a place for Whiteread in that process, outlined by Hal Foster, by which 'postmodern' artists come to fulfil, at least in part, the failed historical project of modernist art.)[20] The public works come to look like those 'lighthouses' described by Walter Benjamin as 'flashing into the future'.[21]

The extraordinary sense of historically acuity that accompanies each of Whiteread's major projects meant that *Monument*, in a space devoted to imperial projects, reflected upon a moment in which those largely invisible, transparent institutions of contemporary ideology embarked upon a new imperial project. This new era of 'gunboat diplomacy' was one played out with helicopter gun-ships, and in the much abused name of 'democracy' rather than of overt imperial aspiration, but it was nonetheless endorsed by the same zealous moral agenda that had sustained good Christian soldiers of the Victorian era. We might see a similar sense of the moment in *Holocaust Memorial*: Whiteread's inaccessible library was unveiled in a moment of resurgence of neo-fascism in Europe, and the rise of political parties attempting to legitimate racial hatred. (Although this time their targets were as likely to be Muslims or Gypsies, as they were Jews.) One of the more visible efflorescences of this trend had manifested in Austria, with the increasing prominence of Jorg Haider's ironically named Freedom Party. But *Holocaust Memorial* could be seen as a more general commentary even as it was geographically and historically specific: reflecting on the constraints placed upon Jewish emigration from central Europe in the 1930s by liberal democracies, and foreshadowing a similar phobia towards the all-purpose bogey of 'asylum seekers' in the new millennium.

Whiteread's most recent project, *Room 101*, cast in the headquarters of the British Broadcasting Corporation (BBC) came at a similar moment of crisis. At its commission *Room 101* seemed to be little more than an acknowledgement by the BBC of its former employee, the writer George Orwell, who had worked in the room during World War Two, and who had used its number as label for the state's ultimate torture chamber in his final novel, *1984*. By the time Whiteread's mould of the room was installed in the casts court of the Victoria & Albert Museum (V&A), it had begun to emblematize more than the historical significance of a writer who had died fifty years before. By mid-2003 it was clear that the BBC Orwell had known – a broadcasting service supported by the state and yet independent of it – was under assault by both commercial pressures and agencies only too fond of the kind of distortions of language and events that Orwell described as typifying totalitarianism. The consequence was a model of broadcasting in which certain concepts – Room 101; Big Brother; the Lottery – that Orwell had included in *1984* to express the horror of state power over the individual had become figures of fun. *Room 101* is a kind of crypt: an interring of public service broadcasting that is also a monument to it. It is the irrecoverable entombment of the BBC's foundational belief in a mass medium that might somehow, simultaneously, 'educate', 'inform' and 'entertain'. What's inside *Room 101* is a Britain rendered obsolete by a state in which things can only get better. Where else for those who believe in what Koolhaas labels 'the luster of renovations'[22] to stuff their phobias – especially the phobic object that is (*was*) public service broadcasting? (For the architecture of which

Koolhaas writes is as much a consequence of government as it is of architects, to the extent that democratic government today is itself a subsidiary function of branded enterprises.) 'Room 101', in both its spatial and conceptual incarnations, was the victim of those who mistake change as a synonym for 'progress'.

This concern with transition, and with what gets thrown out in the process of modernization, means that *Room 101* is a symbol of present and future as much as it is marker for things past. The work measures the BBC's complicity in its degradation, its willingness to be immured articulated through its own debasement of language, its own transformation of concepts of horror into those of momentary entertainment. If *Room 101* is a crypt it is one that houses the form of the human subject which might be produced by the myth of public service broadcasting – that is an active subject, not the consumer beloved of brand managers. But it may be that the BBC is as responsible for that consignment as any of the external influences placed upon it. *Room 101* is not a heterotopia, either in terms of relation or of specificity, (it is, after all, an archive in the archive that is the V&A) but like all of Whiteread's work it solidifies the essence of a moment. Koolhaas remarks that 'myths can be shared, brands husband aura at the mercy of focus groups'.[23] I'd suggest that Whiteread had the opportunity to mark that moment in the BBC's history when it was transformed from myth (the idea that the mass media might objectively foster an autonomous subjectivity) to brand (where the aura of art that might transform 'you' is displaced onto objects of consumption that constitute you).

Central to a group of essays in this collection is a concern with how Whiteread's work 'works': how it functions as sign. What's common to them, whether Shelley Hornstein's invocation of *ostraneniye*, Blake Stimson's idea of 'shimmer' or Susan Lawson's reworking of *infra mince*, is firstly a more sophisticated thinking about the 'uncanny' hesitation that has been the subject of so much critical writing about Whiteread, and secondly, a concern with the structuring of the human subject within language. They raise the questions 'what do those signs that constitute our world mean to us?' and 'how are we constituted, ourselves, by those very signs?' This latter concern is, of course, one commonly ascribed to post-structuralist thought. Concomitant with that is an idea that, if we are no more than composites of signs – constructs of language and ideology that precede us – it may be impossible to intervene and materially change the conditions of our lives. As subjects now, in this space, this moment, we are perhaps both impotent and oblivious. Post-structuralist thinkers as diverse as Foucault and Derrida have rejected this idea of quiescence, but the accusation, unfairly, haunts their critical enterprises.

If Whiteread, as an artist and not a philosopher, is exploring similar questions of how and why signs work in our lives, and what they mean for us, we cannot level a similar accusation of historical passivity. It is the specificity of that concern, manifested in particular works, that informs the second group of essays here. Her oeuvre may be unsentimental in its address, a model of rectitude in its forms and its knowing placement within art's histories, but it is historically charged, relevant to the immediate moment and seems to speak into the future. This charge comes from Whiteread's understanding of the play of language, the way in which a sign is simultaneously not a sign. (After all, what apparently doesn't tell us anything is fundamental to her work; to the way she *does* tell us something.)

In Whiteread's work 'things' collide: past/future; presence/absence; public/private; space/solid; temporary/permanent; aesthetics/historical relevance. It is the complexity of this play between antitheses that, potentially, liberates us from passivity; that, if nothing else, informs us of our condition. Her solid, 'fixed' (yet temporary) monuments speak of our being 'unfixed', our relativity. In this way she is like Bachelard as a thinker, who remarked that 'Man's being is an unfixed being. All expression unfixes him.'[24] Juxtaposed with relativity is our relevance to each other. Whiteread, I think, demands that we recognize the complexity of our mutual entanglement: that is what is embodied in these 'simple' forms. It is this 'simple' call that makes her one of the vital artists of our time. The shimmering patterns of relation, the ever-shifting forces and discourses across time and space, those elements of the archive, determine who we are. Only by recognizing them, by engaging with their complexity, might we begin to see, and inhabit, both our own place in the world, and the spaces and rights of others; who we can't otherwise see, who we brush against at best; at whose forms, when we collide, we can only guess.

33

11   *Untitled (Yellow Bed, Two Parts)* 1991, dental plaster, 167.6 x 68.6 x 35.6cm (66 x 27 x 14in)

CHAPTER 1

REMEMBRANCE OF THINGS PRESENT

JENNIFER R. GROSS

The art historical lens through which I most readily see Rachel Whiteread's stately, silent works surprisingly does not belong to the discipline of sculpture; rather it arises from a tradition in painting. This is the *memento mori*, a term derived from the Latin phrase, 'remember that you must die', and originally a form of classical still life painting developed by the ancient Greeks as a series of visual symbols, to remind the viewer of mortality or death. *Memento mori's* guttering candles, skulls, and trophy animals are the art historical antecedents to Whiteread's resolute mausoleum-slab, and sarcophagus-like forms cast from architectural and household objects. (11)

Vanitas paintings, a form of still life specifically intended to serve as *memento mori*, and popularized by Dutch artists of the seventeenth century, thrived in a culture of unprecedented prosperity founded on religious restraint. These images celebrated the beauty of life and material objects, yet continued to measure the viewer's indulgence against sobering reminders of the fleeting nature of earthly pleasure and the folly of material excess. The charge of the *vanitas* painter was the intimation of unseen life, the primary effect for which Whiteread's work has come to be so well regarded. It is the present moment she enlivens for the viewer, not the past; nor, as many writers have proposed, does her work harbour or proselytize a morbid fixation on loss and death. Her sculptural impressions are distillations of life.

It was Pliny the Elder, writing of Piraikos, a Greek painter of still life and genre paintings during the late fourth to early third century B.C., who first wrote of the history of inanimate objects in art. Piraikos's development of portable works of art, whose subjects were the focused study of things, was a noteworthy departure from the appearance of these items in wall paintings as details in landscape or architectural schemes. Pliny's account also recorded the public delight in these pictures, and their simultaneous disregard by the aestheticians of the day, who believed their content to be of less worth than the grander, well rehearsed themes of historical and mythic narrative.

A still life painting was originally designated in Greek by the term *rhopography*, a depiction of trifling odds and ends lacking narrative content. The disparaging inference in this term was refined in time to indicate an implicit sense of the sordid: *ryparography*. Inherent to the genre was a mannerist form, perhaps influenced by the stylization found in Byzantine mosaics, but more immediately it reflected the cultural penchant for mannerism that pervaded Greek culture during this period.

Xenia, as these still life paintings of food supplies came to be known, continued in Roman times. There were two types of compositions, those displayed in a niche, that suggested a larder or pantry, or those displayed on stone tablets as if in preparation for a dessert table or feast. Numerous examples of these survive in the excavated houses of Herculaneum and Pompeii. In the late medieval era and early Renaissance the evolutions of these niches detailed the spiritual sustenance, of books as well as food, which appended the lives of many portrait subjects. In this context they offered a form of content to the aesthetic record of the person, an imaginative representative of the silent, often contemplative, subject's intellectual and spiritual substance. In addition to their autonomous existence as paintings, these images also appeared on *cassone*, Italian marriage chests, or on the exterior shutters of altarpieces, wardrobes, and cupboards. Displayed in bedchambers, these furnishings were often the first images to be seen by their owner when he or she awoke, setting the correct moral tone for his or her living of the day.

The focused intellectual assault intended by *vanitas* painting began in the fifteenth century in the Low Countries. Rogier van der Weyden's picture of a skull and a chipped brick, *c.* 1450 on a panel of the famous Braque Triptych (in the Louvre) is widely regarded as the first known example of this form. These dramatically lit objects set against an imposing black background were charged with symbolic meaning, and the refined clarity of their *trompe-l'oeil* rendering reinforced their moral import. Whether it was through the depiction of a skull, or worn or broken objects, these compositions evoked contemplative reflection on the precariousness of beauty and time's whimsical sway over human existence.

An intellectual refinement of the *vanitas* form took place in Leyden early in the seventeenth century. Pressured by the persuasive austerity of Calvinism a science of emblems and attributes developed that fell under three primary categories; the contemplative life, the practical life, and the sensual life. It was not until 1650 that the term *Still-leven* was coined. In seventeenth century Dutch, *leven* (life or nature) simply meant 'model', or 'living model'; *still*, of course, meant 'motionless'. Still life paintings, contrary to popular understanding, were not often painted from live or even present subjects but they were carefully composed in reference to earlier artworks, either the artist's own sketches or paintings, or finished works by other painters. Still lifes of game became a popular genre in Holland in the early 1700s. Dead animals, or hunting trophies, were first painted on banquet or scullery tables but soon developed into elaborate schemes that included outdoor country park settings, estate houses, and classical statuary that affirmed the precedents and values asserted in antiquity. These paintings in turn became a form of trophy and were commissioned, bought, and sold with some vigour during this period of conspicuous wealth.[1]

So what is the connection between this tradition in painting and Rachel Whiteread's sculpture? I return to the phrase that lies at the core of the intent behind *vanitas* painting and its antecedents, 'the intimation of unseen life', a phrase effectively turned by the art historian Charles Sterling when writing of the heyday of Dutch still life:

> The sought-after effect is that of a still life which moves us by showing fresh traces of man's presence. The lid of the salt-box is still open, a crust of bread is sticking out of the eggshell. *This intimation of unseen life*, taken by surprise in the silence of the night, comes as a prelude to the calm existence of familiar objects which Claesz and Heda were soon to present in broad daylight.[2]

It is the seeing of the unseen that lies at the heart of Whiteread's aesthetic project. The fresh trace of man's presence has reappeared in her work in various

13 *Untitled (Room)* 1993, plaster, 275 x 300 x 350cm (108 x 118 x 138in)

acter of the volume. Her statement is noteworthy in that it refers to that aspect of place, its oxygen, that one can literally take up into one's body, its life-giving presence. It is this that she wants to preserve, not the aesthetic characteristics of place or space.

While the breath-imbued moment was also the charge of the *memento mori*, Whiteread's 'stilled lives' are distinct from the guttering, perfectly poignant moments arrested in *vanitas* paintings. Her hermetic sculptures do not evoke the recollection of an epic allegory or metaphor. Instead her sculptures confront the viewer with a frame of reference that circles the viewer's reflection back to the object's own unique presence. Unlike the study of a painted image, these forms root the viewer in a physical experience of a specific time and place and raise questions as to their relative relevance.

Beyond the pathos and sensational evocation of themes such as death, entropy, and biography that have been flogged in writings on Whiteread's art, what consistently stands out about her oeuvre is its assertion of positive form made from immaterial spaces. While her early works were sooted and slumped, they remain absolute positive sculptural assertion rather than abject or dissolute forms. Whiteread's field of operation is startlingly conservative at heart: one artist's unwavering commitment to sculpture in the classical tradition which recognizes life in form. Defying the peculiarly English penchant in art and literature to memorialize nostalgia (Gainsborough, Ruskin, Houssman, to name only a few), Whiteread's endeavours reveal her desire to see and know her world, a modern society weighed down by its imperial history and enervated by the scuffed reality of its currently indistinct economic and political status. As she has clearly stated about the room series, which were cast from rooms in derelict industrial buildings or middle class housing: 'All my room pieces – or any architectural pieces I've made – really have to do with observing. There's a sense of puzzlement in just looking at them and thinking: We live in that kind of place. How do we function physically within a place like that? This is definitely what I do when I look at my works. I think about how they affect me physically.'[6] Looked at concisely, Whiteread's sculpture raises the question, 'How do we live here, right here?'; this *here* being both the wider historical and cultural place

41

and the particulars of the aesthetic context.[7] I would argue that this physical self/social-consciousness is the special historical purview of sculpture.

The constant transposition between abstract and representational reference in Whiteread's sculpture is reinforced by the alternate presentation of the work in extremely compressed, and unbounded, exhibition contexts that juggle their reading as both image and form, as intimate or public, as what she likes to call 'in between space.' It is the destabilization of the viewer's expectations and the habitual exchange with familiar surroundings and art that moves the work out of the realm of logic. Instead it enters into the space of the phenomenological experience popularized and aestheticized by the generation of those American artists, working in the 1960s and 1970s, who are most often cited as Whiteread's primary art historical precursors. Whiteread's work hangs in the balance between its recognizable real world imagery and its art-smart vocabulary.

Whiteread is obviously informed when it comes to both ancient and modern art history. In fact, she has consistently acknowledged the art historical precedents to her work, and unapologetically pays homage to them through her words as well as through her re-visitation of images, materials, and forms. When asked to evaluate her relationship to Minimalist precedents, Whiteread replied:

> I try to make things look easy when, in fact, they're incredibly difficult. Someone like Serra does this as well. He uses these extraordinary masses, yet the best pieces look completely effortless. My response to sculpture is often physical, the physical way in which you look at something. Serra is a perfect example of an artist who does that. He changes your perception of how you put one foot in front of the other when you're walking around or through something. What happens is that you think about your physical place in the world.[8]

Rosalind Krauss, in her watershed essay 'Sculpture in the Expanded Field', reviewed the commonly accepted definition of modernist sculpture in order to contrast it to a post-modernist practice she felt was developing at that time:

> I would submit that we know very well what sculpture is. And one of the things we know is that it is a historically bounded category and not

a universal one. As is true of any other convention, sculpture has its own internal logic, its own set of rules, which, though they can be applied to a variety of situations, are not themselves open to very much change. The logic of sculpture is a commemorative representation. It sits in a particular place and speaks in a symbolical tongue about the meaning or use of that place. (...) Because they thus function in relation to the logic of representation and marking, sculptures are normally figurative and vertical, their pedestals an important part of the structure since they mediate between actual site and representational sign.[9]

Krauss went on in that essay to identify the expanded 'post-modern' field of sculptural operation as one that exists beyond the negative condition of sculpture, that which is the sum of an additive equation incorporating non-landscape and non-architecture. Defying the vein of pure negativity that modernist sculpture had become, artists such as Walter De Maria, Michael Heizer, and Robert Smithson had problematized the oppositions that apparently existed between landscape and architecture. The resulting 'earthworks' operated on the periphery, literally, in some instances, mapping the terrain of this newly defined three-dimensional field.

Two generations later, Whiteread, after being trained under sculptors such as Edward Allington, Eric Bainbridge, Antony Gormley, and Alison Wilding[10] embraced the modernist definition of sculpture and all its negativity. Impressed by the resolute force inherent in the austere forms of American minimalist and post-minimalist works by Carl Andre, Bruce Nauman and Donald Judd, Whiteread seems to have picked up the phenomenological ball where it was dropped in the late 1970s. There, at the outer limit of the expanded field defined by Krauss and excavated by the likes of Heizer, Smithson and Serra, she is addressing particular places and engendering a dialogue about the meaning or use of that place.

Beginning with her very first works, Whiteread was invested in exploring traditional artistic methods and forms. The transition of her practice from landscape painting to sculpture even traversed the mediating field of the relief frieze. In contrast to a generation of artists who were encouraged to shop, display, or farm out

43

14   *Valley* 1990, plaster and glass, 95.3 x 185.4 x 96.5cm (37¹/₂ x 73 x 38in)

15 *Ether* 1990, plaster, 109.2 x 87.6 x 204.5cm (43 x 34$\frac{1}{2}$ x 80$\frac{1}{2}$in)

the labour end of their conceptual processes, Whiteread delved into the third dimension personally, up to her elbows in casting, carving, and modelling, the triumvirate core of traditional sculptural practice.[11] She has consistently been at pains to reveal these processes in order to demystify the aura and the artifice of the work, as well as her role as creator. She invites the viewer to see through her work as art, not across its surface, and to know how the resulting image was created. Much like the objects in a still-life painting, the intimation of life comes from image as well as form but Whiteread asserts the presence of the sculpture. What the viewer sees is the negative image of a familiar form. What he or she physically encounters is an object that remains slightly out of the reach of cognitive definition. The 'madeleine' inspired experience of culture and history only goes so far before it short circuits, leaving the viewer with a slightly disconcerting recognition and engagement with a form that is wholly new and which is asserted through its presentation as art.

Rather than simply embrace the expanded field established for art in the 1970s, Whiteread engages the viewer, who has learned the post-modernist spectrum of broader possibility for art, and brings them back to a more traditional starting point for an encounter with sculpture. No longer needing to operate in defiance of the system that inescapably holds up the reading and experience of her work, Whiteread's objects and monuments are consistently sited within the historical field of art and their familiar forms quickly move the viewer from this touchstone, the luring and particular purview of art, on to new experiences of confounding confrontation; both monumental intimacy as with *House*, 1992, and alienating familiarity as with her casts of household objects. These distilled forms reveal the artist's non-objective exposure of universal experience through creative process.

It is Whiteread's commitment to revealing artistic method, the seductive elements in her industrial material choices, and her endeavour to marry them to a painstakingly considered casting process, that draws the viewer closer to her art. The resulting forms have inviting, accessible surfaces that celebrate the happy marriage of the manual industry and industrial technology that make her work possible. In a sense Whiteread appears to be helping sculpture come clean, after a number of years of apologetic self-deprecation. Whiteread is persevering under the conviction that form is the end to its own means for an artist and that this is such an inherently lively endeavour that the viewer will be compelled into their own engaged physical and psychological experience. Her modernism is one in which image and form are clearly revealed not as being the hermetic ends for art but as touchstones to reassert the viewer's conceptual and physical embrace of a world from which they feel frighteningly disengaged. The sculptures stand as evidence of Whiteread's archaeological survey of the present, a form of public service not anticipated by the viewer, and in distinct contrast to the tendency for minimalist sculptors to create aesthetic untouchables out of familiar materials.

Whiteread's most recent projects, using transparent resins to create public monuments, continue to assert this aspect of her enterprise. Beginning with *House*, Whiteread was introduced to the tradition of sculpture as public monument and to the responsibilities and challenges inherent in making an object whose intention is to engage an expectant public. For an artist to assert and insert form into culture, even when it was a skein of a pre-existing piece of that culture, proved highly controversial. The history of the monument and of the object, in this case the house, overwhelmed the public's primary physical experience of the work with archaeological and political content. Solid form in this instance, and again later with her *Holocaust Memorial*, 2000, in Vienna, embodied the site's historical meaning for most viewers.

47

Whiteread's experiments with transparency (16) revive the early modernist endeavour to reveal or remove the interiority of sculptural form and the audience's anticipation of, or search into, form for meaning that is the bailiwick of the public monument. While early modern sculptors had previously used polished surfaces to reflect back to viewers the world in which their work resided, it was Marcel Duchamp who most famously used glass as a surface unfettered by optical finality or illusionistic resolution to confirm the perpetual 'makingness' inherent in visual experience through his *Large Glass*, 1915–23.[12] Casting *Water Tower*, 1998, the cast of a water tower on a New York rooftop, in resin, allowed Whiteread to make a monumental public sculpture that could be seen through and effect what she called 'something that was more like an intake of breath' as an aesthetic experience.[13] The trans-

16 *Untitled (Clear Slab)* 1992, rubber, 198.1 x 78.7 x 10.2cm (78 x 31 x 4in)

parent material allowed an optical encounter that transformed the originating form from which it was cast. While the presence of that object was evoked by its location, no history could be hung on the resulting light-refracting form. During the day the sculpture was diffused in light and at night it was re-asserted as negative form, as a smudge of darkness, a deeper emptiness in a dark sky.

This denial of optical surety confirms Whiteread's belief in phenomenological information, the kind of knowledge that drives how we see. With this work, and with *Monument*, 2001, the viewer could literally look at the world through her art. *Water Tower* intimated the life of its originating form without being confined as its record. Close up its surface showed the imprint of the original water tower's wall but from the streets of SoHo this detailing was invisible, and the form looked like a massing of solidified liquid. The sculpture's actual configuration was not a physical rendering of a surface view of an object but was the record of the surface of its un-seeable volume, the interior surface casting of a void that Whiteread asserted as a solid. Whiteread had cast the image of the unseen.

49

The making of *Monument* for Trafalgar Square in London in 2001 provided Whiteread with the opportunity to further develop the issues of legibility and content raised by *Water Tower*. Whiteread was asked to address an empty monumental plinth that is permanently located on Trafalgar Square. The pedestal begged to be filled by a traditional trophy figure or ornament that would commemorate a past event or articulate the artist's cultural insight. This prescription had already been filled by the artists who had preceded Whiteread in this scheme, so she moved to effect an alternative experience. *Monument* is a replica in clear resin of the empty plinth. Set on top of the original granite plinth as its 'ghostly mirror image', *Monument* reflected the buildings, people, and traffic that encircled the square. Light coursed across its surfaces and into the transparent form causing its image to change color and fade in and out of view in response to the changeable English sky. A built emblem of contemporary culture, a monumental form made by a young living artist through modern industrial manufacturing techniques and materials, *Monument* managed to avoid the limits of the self-referential life of a pure modernist marker. The viewer looked through and around it as its haunting presence created a focal point, without providing any fixed meaning or interpretation of the historically and socially charged location. The work commemorated art and life without recourse to traditional representation and, when its term of service on Trafalgar Square drew to a close, it was hauled off this originating site, given a new base, and awaits installation in a location that is yet to be determined. Here, it continues to reflect place, acting as an enabling lens onto a new site and an ever unfolding present.

Memento mori, many of which included architectural monuments, and commemorative public sculpture, are primary examples of traditional art forms as moral practice. Artists working in these traditions, as well as their patrons, believed in religious and cultural ideals that they wished to recall in their viewers. The forms they made were imbued with external imperatives, premeditated logic. Stepping out in the world in which she lives, Whiteread encourages us – as well as herself – not to see beyond our real means, but rather to see what is right in front of our noses. The ideal she wishes us to apprehend is *carpe diem*, the seizing of the present. There is no mystery or mastery in her work but the present interface of life and matter at her hand. Her subjects are as simple as those of the French still-life painter of the eighteenth century, Jean-Baptiste-Siméon Chardin's, the stilled faces of the world around her. Like Chardin, Whiteread literally pulls out the surface and spaces of her world and from this humble store she casts for us objects through which we encounter unremarkable yet significant reflections, of our presence in time, our unseen life. A pleasant by-product of Whiteread's revealing these elements through form is that we see the trace of our presence, of the life we are in, reflected in them too, of the life we are standing in next to her *memento mori*.

CHAPTER 2

MATTERS IMMATERIAL
On the Meaning of Houses and the Things Inside Them

SHELLEY HORNSTEIN

And art exists that one may recover the sensation of life;

it exists to make one feel things, to make the stone *stony*.

Victor Shklovsky

Does it matter that things in our everyday life are material? What is the relationship

of a thing to an idea, a house to a home? Rachel Whiteread makes things matter.

She takes objects we think we know – a bed, a table – and makes them into some-

thing material that we no longer recognize. Not only is she after defamiliarizing the

familiar, she heightens the materiality of the thing, making it seem to be more than

what it is in its physical form. More, yet never more physically; that is, never more

than its original mass. How is more not really more, yet more so? In what way do

Whiteread's *House* and her domestic 'furniture' pieces, such as such as *Mantle*,

1988 (19); *Yellow Leaf,* 1989 (20) or *Untitled (Wardrobe)*, 1994 (17), reclaim place as

something more than the just the object in situ? I would argue that this reclama-

tion of familiarity is a testament to the weightiness and place of the object through

the doubling of the original. It is through Whiteread's trademark casting tech-

niques that these objects demand attention, and it is this *demanding* that I want to

observe at close quarters. What is it about these objects that compels us to respond

and take notice, particularly if their everydayness might suggest we pass them by?

What is it about the materiality of the work of Rachel Whiteread that is important?

Take *House*. Whiteread sought to make a cast of a house. Its formative model,

Ghost (18), was an 'object' exhibited in a museum-like space.[1] As a cast of a living

room of a Victorian house installed inside yet another architectural structure,

17 *Untitled (Wardrobe)* 1994, plaster and glass, 180 x 125 x 46cm (70^7/$_8$ x 49^1/$_4$ x 18^1/$_8$in)

Whiteread played with the museum's generic institutional space as background to the highly personalized and private residential space of the home. Of that project, she says, 'When I made *Ghost*, I was interested in relocating a room, relocating a space, from a small domestic house into a big concrete anonymous place, which is what the museums have done all over the world for years and years.'[2]

On the heels of *Ghost* and its substantive international success, *House*, an even more ambitious project, was already in its conceptual phase. Site, in tandem with the qualities of mass and materiality, were critical components for the work, as is always the case for Whiteread's projects. After several unsuccessful explorations of several north and east London neighbourhoods, Whiteread, assisted by Artangel director, James Lingwood, was able finally to acquire a temporary lease for a Victorian terrace at 193 Grove Road in Bow, east London. Work began after several official paperwork delays in August 1993. On November 23 of the same year Whiteread was the recipient of the coveted Turner Prize, and on the very same day, Tower Hamlets councillors voted in favour of the demolition of *House*, effective immediately. (Though the structure did not come down until January 1994.) As Lingwood aptly remarked, 'It was an incendiary combination.'[3] This necessarily fuelled the media circus that resulted and catapulted the notoriety – one might even suggest with caution: the 'sacredness' – of the project to the world beyond the Bow neighbourhood.[4]

While Rachel Whiteread's urban interventions, in particular, trouble by the nature of their insertions as well as by their subject matter – critical to the discourses we enter into when we experience the works or even consider them through photographs – I want to argue that the sequencing of the thoughtful process of engaging with the work must begin with an understanding of the type of materiality each piece is in conjunction with its *placement*. I am not suggesting that each and every artwork is to be understood solely through the lenses of matter and place above all else, though the suggestion is tempting. At least for the purposes of Rachel Whiteread's considered observations of *House* and of house furniture, materiality and place – as they are made known to us through the process of casting and the subsequent location, placement and intervention in space of the cast object – remain the central themes of her work upon which all other reflections are brought to bear.

53

18   *Ghost* 1990, plaster on steel frame, 269 x 356 x 318cm (106 x 140 x 125in)

House categorically refutes the notion of buying into a nostalgic enterprise. The mere reference to the term 'house' as opposed to 'home' announces this position. As a monument to the idea of 'house', this work challenges concepts of community, place and security. Its status as place is continually confronted. Its physical site problematizes the politics of geography and location that necessarily lead to protracted discussions about identity and nationhood. The qualities of nostalgia often associated with imagining home are rejected forthright, indeed repelled. To force this trajectory of thought is one of the ways in which *House* subverts any idea that where we live is a simple and comfortable, even neutral, territory. Whiteread's project, through its (eventually) successful battle to get built and – after protests and media events – its unsuccessful battle to continue to stand, shored up at every moment the disruptive nature of architecture in place.

What we are left with is a challenge to any concept of 'house'. In fact, this house is not a house. This house might be considered uncanny. Uncanny, that is, in the sense Freud suggested. That is, this *House*, by Rachel Whiteread, is in a class of those things we consider frightening: as a result, this object leads us back to what feels comfortable, what is known and familiar.[5] The conundrum is that we cannot determine what is known and familiar about this house because it is entirely unknown and cannot ever be known – for entrance to it is prohibited and we are defeated by any attempt to enter regardless. It is full and its insides – or, its 'fullness' – are now on the outside. The internal mass of the house has *de facto* become its exoskeleton forming a barrier, a kind of – in this case – opaque cage, that excludes penetration and protects the mythical interior.

Taken all too lightly most of the time, architecture – an object, a frame, a shell, a placemaker – is often ignored. Whiteread's house-that-is-not-a-house demonstrates this powerfully. We carry on our daily activities always in, through, around architectural spaces yet we are almost indifferent to them. In fact our lives are modulated, mediated and moderated by the spaces of architectural configurations (walls, streets, pathways, corridors, roofs, and so on) yet we would be hard-pressed to remember precisely the dimensions or details of a place we frequent such as the office, or the home. In a way, this is a good thing. The shapes in which we function become moulded to our projects, our patterns. We wear the architecture of our everyday lives like a skin with the expectation that it will always be there to protect us and continue to provide the shell within which we become defined.

Rachel Whiteread's *House* is all that Freud conveys when he discusses the unusual semantics of the terms *heimlich* and *unheimlich*. In the first sense, *heimlich* conveys the familiar, or the known. But curiously, the other meaning of the word, *heimlich*, is that which is unknown, or that which is secret. To further complicate matters, the term which is, in principle, its opposite, *unheimlich*, usually conveys that which is unknown and unfamiliar, but also that which is unconcealed or unsecret. Therefore, Freud's argument is that *unheimlich* or the 'uncanny' is that which is concealed, but also that which is known and familiar. Two opposite interpretations that overlap, that double, as one.

If doubling those interpretations gets at the essence of Whiteread's objective for her piece, then *House*, we could say, is rich in its connotations of intimacy and the personal as well as it is rich and controversial about all that we share as public and familiar. Whiteread ensures that this doubled reading is argumentative, political and bold. But her work at base is about doubling as a process best understood through the experience of the object, that is, the material object she makes for us to experience. The doubling principle in her work, then, needs closer examination. Of the diverse and numerous writings about her work, the technique she employs as her standard is often mentioned, but never explored in detail. In each of Whiteread's projects there is a heightened consideration of the material process, of the hand process lost to the process of the multiple (hinted at by the process of casting). It is a process, through the subtle variances she introduces from project to project, that in the end defines her work. She has been hailed as someone who casts, whose work is about casting and whose work is about loss (of the object, thus absent or reversed). But more than this, it seems to me that Whiteread's projects are always the objects doubled, or the spaces doubled, through the process of the mould and its cast.

Architecture that was once on a site is no longer on a site; yet even while it stood prior to demolition, *House* qua house, while no longer a house in fact, actually was. The original house was removed and replaced – but not exactly. This non-

19   *Mantle* 1988, plaster and glass, 61 x 120 x 53cm (24 x 47¹/₄ x 20⁷/₈in)

sensical reconfiguration of the familiar house was now proposed as a deformity of the real. What is the casting technique? Casting is a technique to 'form [*an object*] into a shape, by pouring it when melted or soft into a mould, where it is allowed to cool or harden.'[6] The cast for *House* was the house at Grove Road itself (its walls, floors, staircases, in short, the surfaces of its complete interior). Filled up with liquid concrete, the private insides (of the outside) registered the impression of the surfaces, nooks and crannies, onto its surfaces. The outside house that served as the mould was then demolished. *House* was a giant dental impression, a fossilized remain as much as it was the complement to the frame or exterior. To think about the double of the cast is to think about the properties that define what we know to be our objects of material culture.

Rachel Whiteread makes sculpture but the material object she makes is the object created from a mould. Put another way, without this technique, without the primacy of the mould around 'real' things, we would not have work, at least not any of the work we currently know, by Whiteread. Unlike sculptors generally categorized as those who traditionally either build up (in terracotta, wax, plaster), or carve by breaking down a monolithic material (marble, granite, whittled or carved wood), Whiteread has no object she initially creates. Instead she uses the objects of our material culture as her point of departure. By taking the imprint of found objects, and specifically large-scale and architectural, architectural-related or architectonic objects (plinths, water towers, bookshelves, furniture, houses), she is commenting on the deeply rooted relationship we hold to objects integral to our everyday lives.

By framing the objects with a mould, she is framing objects for us to consider, much as frames identify and highlight works in a museum. Our gaze shifts from the everyday to a heightened experience of the object in its newly-articulated form and place (even when that place is on the same site it originally occupied in its 'original' site). In the same way, Whiteread frames and exposes what she wants us to pay attention to and separate from the everyday so that we take notice. The casting process, no matter what the material used, allows her to do just this. And the detail and refinement she devotes to researching this process are exemplary. Take, for example, a description of the technique used for *Monument,* 2001:

20 *Yellow Leaf* 1989, plaster, formica and wood, 150 x 73.7 x 94cm (59 x 29 x 37in)

Monument is a replica of the stone plinth on which it stands cast in water-clear resin and inverted on top of the original. The mould was not made directly from the plinth as it is a listed monument and therefore it is not possible to take a cast of it. The mould was constructed to the same dimensions. Approximately 11 tons of the material was used to make it. It is cast in two hollow sections which sit one on top of the other. Each section was stage poured over several hours into an aluminium mould. It was demoulded after 30 hours and continued to cure over the next week. The interior was filled and sanded where marks had been left by the mould, and then sprayed with a clear lacquer... It took four months to construct the mould... The making of the plinth was delayed by the technical difficulties involved in casting such a large volume of resin. A long period of research and development was necessary to determine the right material and casting technique. Some of the particular difficulties were: the varying thicknesses of different parts of the mould; the high temperatures generated inside the mould by the curing of the resin; the tendency of resin to contract as it hardens.[7]

Questions she is exploring through her technique are centred on some of the following formal qualities: what is the nature of tactility and weight in an object? Through the process of taking an impression, literally, what is the imprint left in the material that serves as a fossilization under pressure? Does casting try to shape the object that will then disappear? And in that process, something is always being lost: inside or outside. Rachel Whiteread renews the conventions of casting in two different ways: first, she creatively investigates new materials – resin, rubber, dental plaster, and re-examines ancient materials used in casting such as concrete. Second, she plays with the methods of casting and the idea of shaping a 'thing'. Instead of moulding the object as object and then filling that mould with resin, for example, she creates a cast to frame the object and then fills the space between the mould and the object with resin, rubber or another material. Her frames of space that are shaped on the inside by the absence of the object once the mould and the interiorized object is removed, constitute the nature of her practice.

Another strategy she uses to shape 'things' is somewhat more traditional to the extent that she shapes a mould around the object she identifies, say a mattress, and then eventually fills the empty space created by the mould occupied earlier by that object, the mattress. But defiantly, she transforms the tactile knowledge we all carry of a mattress (soft, pliable, bouncy and dense) in an almost subversive move: rubber and high density foam replace the quality so familiar to us (21, 22). Furthermore, she saturates the new material with an amber hue and straddles the mattress halfway up a wall. Its function is unclear; its familiarity rendered foreign.

Not only does Whiteread articulate casts in a variety of materials, but she does so to capitalize on mass and weight. Above all, the works address presence by mass and weight. The contents of her pieces never really move. The subjects of those works are moved, occasionally, either to move locations within a house, or to move from one house to another, or to move out of the house into someone else's house, or finally, to the trash – its dead end. In all cases, however, movement is limited, rare, and not an association we would make with the object. For that matter, *House* is perhaps the quintessentially stable, rock-solid symbol of place and endurance in a collective of houses: the neighbourhood. We could say that virtuality has shaped city life in novel ways that alter the dimensional comprehension of propinquity. Western society has devalued rock-solidity or at least our symbols of architectural stability have shifted. That which is fluid, partial, fleeting and above-all, virtual, qualifies that which is valued. Cities, in the ongoing anxiety and crisis management of speed and progress measured by the scopic measuring stick of modernity, nego-tiate movement. Virtuality and media explorations disrupt and extend any urban perspectives we may have held dear and instead, traditional spaces seem to have been expanded virtually beyond the architectonics of the common shelter and prim-itive hut. Indeed *House* by Whiteread, as a result of its weightiness, seems to har-ness virtual energy in order to revisit the pace of the standstill. This is a return to the notion of monumentality best understood through the mystery of the great monuments of the past – we can think of the Parthenon, the Colosseum, the

61

21 *Untitled (Amber Double Bed)* 1991,
rubber and high density foam, 119.4 x 137.2 x 104.1cm (47 x 54 x 41in)

22   *Untitled (Amber Bed)* 1991, rubber, 129.5 x 91.4 x 101.6cm (51 x 36 x 40in)

Pyramids. Each of these continues to mystify in part by its design but largely as a result of its scale and weight. This weightiness or monumentality marks the material presence of *House*, and is sensed in the spirit of the furniture units as well.

When we think of a house or the furniture elements that are requisite to it, we are hard-pressed to consider a house for its *houseness*. Rather, we are deadened by its convention in our everyday lives. In fact, to perceive a house and its function from the inside is not an active process. We are far more accustomed to admiring house façades and their concatenation on streets; their interiors are private spaces for which invitations are necessary. As for our own house interiors, we know them all too well, or do we? Rachel Whiteread's primordial tale, the one that resonates above all else, seems to be the presence of this object, this house. It is something that is voluminous, solid and massive, in the way of something else, immovable, incomprehensible. It is strangely familiar yet ultimately unfamiliar. It is an expression of art that exists, as best stated in this circumstance by Shklovsky, 'that one may recover the sensation of life; it exists to make one feel things, to make the stone *stony*.'[8] What Shklovsky argues for is an ability to begin to recognize the object in front of our eyes because until the time that this object was 'declared' art it was an object we never saw. We are thrown into an 'automatism of perception' as he suggests, that is remedied only by art that succeeds by describing a process in detail through the act of *ostraneniye* or 'defamiliarization'.[9] While these Formalist theories were first written in 1917, they are, to my mind, the most apt way of understanding the specificity of Rachel Whiteread's *House* and furniture. And it is not a simple technique that Shklovsky offers. It is one that is not simply about naming but naming parts never before named. Shklovsky uses Tolstoy's example of 'pricking the conscience' with aplomb. He quotes from *War and Peace* in order to demonstrate how Tolstoy, among others, transformed meanings by replacing common associations attached to rituals and customs, particularly those religious in nature, by seeing things and describing them outside the parameters of their accepted contexts. As a result, his work was considered sacrilegious to many. But the process, employed by other Russian Formalists such as Boris Tomashevsky for his analyses of Swift and Pushkin, signalled the wake-up call for considering the art itself. In other words, the defamiliar-

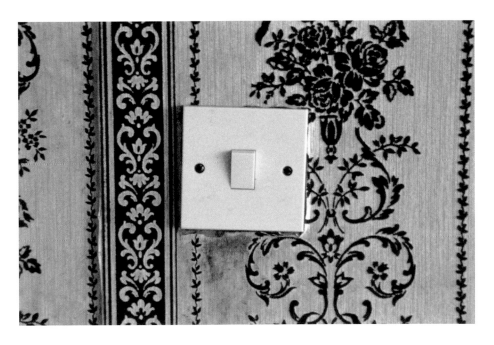

23 *Light Switches* 1996–98, two R-type photographs, each: 20.3 x 25.4cm (8 x 10in)

24   Detail of *Untitled (Room)*

ization process shifted the attention back to the object itself. Our previously skewed view of the known object (a house, a bathtub, a table) is shaken into an awareness, indeed a new awareness, of the ordinary, and the object draws attention to itself. Suddenly the details of the mundane (electrical outlets, lightswitches (23), letterboxes (24), windows, walls) focus our attention on what we had never seen, and particularly on the materiality of the house, its *stoniness* (or concreteness).

With this deliberate act to awaken our automatized perceptions, Whiteread highlights the pieces and parts of the whole that eventually contribute to how we perceive the content. And while the Modernist duality of form and content can never be separated – nor should we even think of these two categories as the governing concepts in considering works of art – there is, nevertheless, a visceral response to the tactility of the material: its presence and sheer imagined (and at least, visual) weight wholly engages our eye and sharpens our focus on the nature of materiality altogether. In a deft move, Whiteread reconfigured that strategy: for *House,* she used the real house as the mould and filled up the inside. Once the outside was demolished, the inside stood, bare and revealed. The bipolarity of the process requires that one of the two parts is removed from its place, rendering the notion of place placeless. Yet her work can easily be seen as a completion of the circle since we're only given one half through which we're asked to imagine the whole. Concrete fills up all the spaces of the inside and when the outside walls are demolished, when that mould is peeled away, *House* stands alone with all its insides declared: a solid mass of inside, out. We behold that which is never valorized by others: a denuded place, a house stripped bare of its *houseness* with its entrails revealed curiously inside the outside now gone. All the cultural values – and secrets – expressed in a home and invisible to the outsider, are sedimented in concrete, at once almost erased and preserved in what could have been taken as a monument – at least while *House* stood – to the lost object. Even though highly visible, the standing object, flayed of its protective skin, is no longer in sight. We have lost *sight* of the initial object, the relationship of *House* to demolition and later, in a doubling of that destruction when *House* was demolished, we lost *site* as well.

67

25   *Model of Untitled (Wall)* 1999,
dimensions of full-size work 312 x 894 x 10.2cm (123 x 352 x 4in)

CHAPTER 3

SENSITIVE SKIN

infra mince and *différance* in the work of Rachel Whiteread

SUSAN LAWSON

It is almost a commonplace amongst those whose task it is to write essays such as these – to make links, sometimes obvious, sometimes tenuous, between artworks and 'theories' – to suggest that Rachel Whiteread's work embodies or uses or implies in some way the most basic premises of Jacques Derrida's concept of 'deconstruction'. Her work, simply put, destabilizes the classic dichotomy of presence and absence in which presence is the privileged term and, bringing both to mind at once, holds them in the balance.

Aside from the implication that visual art can 'illustrate' a 'theory', an implication which would tend to reduce an artwork's visual and bodily impact to an aside and which ignores the irreducibility of the physical to the word or concept (a problem which concerns all art criticism of this type), in this particular case – that of Whiteread and Derrida – there is a further complication. 'Deconstruction' was conceived, at least originally, if there can be an 'originally' in Derridean thought, as an approach to an already existing and usually canonical text, in order to expose what had been repressed, belied or forgotten in the formation of that text. To do Derrida's approach any true justice, then, we would have to take Whiteread's works to be 'visual deconstructions' of the objects from which she casts. Aside from the dubious slide from language to object and from textual to visual, the idea of 'deconstructing' a bathtub, for example, or a brick wall (for such is the focus of this essay) would no doubt have Derrida banging his head against one. Alternatively we might take Whiteread's works themselves to be 'texts', and deconstruct them. By this token we might deconstruct any piece of art and Whiteread's work would hold no special privilege for the method.

Yet it remains that there is something about Whiteread's work that, for want of a better word, *reminds* people – myself included – of Derrida's thinking. For me, perversely perhaps, it was the physical and psychological impact of seeing Whiteread's work that led me to want to understand the nature of its relationship to Derrida's ideas, in the hope that delving deeper into such theoretical concerns might illuminate a bodily reaction.

I had already seen Whiteread's solo show at Anthony d'Offay Gallery (October 1998 - January 1999) in which the piece I plan to focus on – *Untitled (Wall)* – was installed, when, almost two years later, at the exhibition 'Between Cinema and A Hard Place' at Tate Modern, 2000, I stumbled, claustrophobic, out of an Ilya Kabakov labyrinth and, already disorientated, came face to façade with *Ghost*, Whiteread's full size cast of a living room. I must have looked like I had seen one – a ghost that is – because the piece had such an immediate and bodily effect on me, a shock which I can't now describe any better than to say I felt slapped in the face. It was a sort of whiting out in the brain, a shift sideways, a draining of blood from the head.

It was only in retrospect that it struck me what it was about *Ghost* that disturbed me both physiologically and psychologically, and it wasn't only that I couldn't get in. It wasn't only that it reminded me of bed-sits I had lived and loved in, and that the things that had gone on in such bed-sits were left to me only in frayed and faded memories, though it was that too. If you'd never fallen in and out of love in a bed-sit, and if you weren't getting progressively worried about your age, these things wouldn't have upset you. Rather, it was the skin of it; the absolute exteriority. What you get is what you see. *Ghost* is a piece that leaves you reeling in its utter disdain, its forlornness: its refusal to allow you any more than a front. (While other viewers of the piece have commented on the cracks in its walls, which allow a glimpse of the interior, *Ghost*'s monumental force had affected me such that I had not noticed them, and my experience remains one of impenetrability.) It seemed to me, looking back, that it is the outermost surface of a Whiteread that holds its power and perhaps, its content.

It was then, too, that I started thinking back on the other work I've mentioned, *Untitled (Wall)*, which had at the time impressed itself on my memory but had not, then, struck me as being in any special way distinctive in her oeuvre. For sure it *was* distinctive, in that it was the only work of Whiteread's that I had seen which exhibited the mould at the same time as the cast taken from it, and the only one as well that showed its framing structure explicitly. But it was only on seeing *Ghost* that the particular pertinence of *Wall* seemed to be revealed. Where the impact of *Ghost*'s surface rendered its depths almost insignificant, *Wall* was surface itself.

Wall, a temporary installation, consisted of a cast of the wall of the rear gallery, set back from the wall by a couple of feet. Behind the cast the wooden framework that supported it was exposed, a structure much like the frames that make up the internal walls of your average new-build house before the plasterboard is fixed. Between the wall and the cast of the wall there was formed a sort of corridor. Walking down it, to my left the wall, with its indents where the grouting was, to the right of me the same 'bricks' in reverse, and where there should have been channels, protrusions. The cast ran around two sides of the gallery, parallel to the two walls and, where the gallery wall cut across the corner in a diagonal, so too did the cast of the wall follow, echoing even the achitecture's irregularity. (The maquette of the installation (25), differs from the realized piece in that it shows two false walls set in space rather than the gallery wall and its cast).

The wall and its cast thus formed, between them, a corridor. (In light of Whiteread's nod to Bruce Nauman in works such as *Untitled (Six Spaces)*, 1994, one cannot avoid a possible reference here to the American artist's corridor works, most famously *Walk with Contrapposto*, 1968, which itself references art history in Nauman's mimicry, as he walks down the corridor, of the classical pose struck by Michelangelo's sculpture of David.) Whiteread's 'corridor' seemed to me not only to form an impossible space (I will return to this idea) but also, in retrospect, to underscore certain concerns of Whiteread's oeuvre in general. The fact that in this piece both the cast and the mould are held in actual, spatial relation to each other, and the fact that the framing structure is readily admitted, suddenly seemed to me to be both an exposition of, even the key to, the rest of her work and to her thinking as a whole. It was, if you will, a meta-Whiteread, in the same sense that meta-language reveals the machinations of language beneath its seemly surface.

71

With *Ghost*, on the contrary, the viewer could well, as I did, assume that the work is solid. The details of the materials however, 'plaster on steel frame', reveal instead that the piece itself is a shell, held up with a framework presumably similar (though of a different material) to the one exposed in *Wall*. In a sense what we see is merely cladding, and its thickness is only relevant in a practical sense – in order to make the piece stand up in a gallery without being too heavy. Plasterers who number amongst my friends can confirm that, solid, *Ghost* would probably bring down the house.

Crucially, as I've said, in *Wall*, the cast-mould relationship is exhibited. But since the only relation between a cast and a mould is indexical – the cast must touch the mould intimately to exist – this is the relation foremost in your mind precisely as you walk between them. As your body separates them (and I can't help but think of those embarrassed people walking gingerly through the doorway formed by a naked Marina Abramović and Ulay in the performance piece *Imponderabilia*, 1977) you are wholly aware that they have been pressed very tightly together.

Is it for this reason that the space in *Wall* seemed to be impossible, or at least impossibly *thin*? It is difficult to pinpoint where the bricks ended and the cast began. Instead of walking between a presence and its reverse, or, more accurately, down an absence slung between two presences, walking through *Wall* was like skirting the very border between the two.

It is this observation that will lead me down the by now rather muddy Derrida trail. As I've said, it's all too tempting to talk, either flippantly or deeply, of Whiteread's works in terms of absences and presences and their reversal – and such observations would be crucial in discussing for example her book works such as *Untitled (Pulp)* (26), which hint at the writing of the un-written, the gaps between words, the unsaid that is repressed in the writing of History. And it is all too compelling to leap from here straight into Derrida's (non) notion of deconstruction, especially in light of architecture's love affair with deconstruction[1] and Whiteread's architectural structures.

Bearing in mind the architectural quality of Whiteread's work, it is worth noting briefly here that architecture students are often taught, following the master-

26   *Untitled (Pulp)* 1999, plaster, polystyrene and steel in 5 sections
168 x 180 x 26cm (66$^{1}/_{8}$ x 70$^{7}/_{8}$ x 10$^{1}/_{4}$in)

Modernist Le Corbusier, to design from the plan up, that is, to sculpt space itself. In this thinking the walls are merely the tools that allow space itself to be sculpted. When a building is actually built, these walls have solidity and must be accounted for in material terms; however when you draw a plan the lines representing the walls are themselves perceived as absences. It is the shape of the rooms – the sculpted voids – that counts. So Whiteread's rooms (in *Ghost* and *House*) express exactly what the Modernist architect envisions before s/he has to deal with such tedious matters as breezeblock.

Yet what is interesting to me and what seems to be foregrounded in *Wall* is not just the straightforward dichotomy 'absence/presence', but rather the point precisely between them, just like the forward slash I've had to use to express this. Obviously, every artwork has an edge – forget art, every *object* has an edge – a point at which presence stops and absence begins.[2] Yet with Whiteread, this boundary-skin is always so heavily marked or even tainted (as in the book works where the colour of the pages has come off on the cast) that it warrants much closer investigation.

The solidified void that is *Ghost* might well be read as a metaphor for memories trapped within the unconscious. We might also say, in relation to Derrida (as I hope to show), that works such as *Ghost* render visible the *absence that counts*. Crucially, however, it is the point at which this 'solid void' or 'present absence' meets the void in which it sits, the air of the gallery, that is not only inscribed but itself circumscribes the work: inscribed with the traces of the walls from which *Ghost* has been cast, and, as limit and visible edge, circumscribing both the artwork and our visual access to it. It is all, in fact, that the viewer can see: in that sense then, the surface might be seen to constitute the artwork itself.

For Derrida the concept of *différance* embodies the originary difference (or specifically, as he would have it, the '~~originary~~ difference'[3]), deferral and indeed dissension that not only separates any *it* from what *it* is not, but also constitutes *it* by virtue of not being *what it is not*. If I may attempt the impossible (before continuing): to reduce *différance* to two or so sentences (and already I'm paring the 'excess' from the idea in order to 'capture' it, already I'm repressing those characteristics of *différance* that don't fit my use of it as a tool), we might say that there are at the very least three deferrals/differences at play within Derrida's understanding of *différance* that may be tactically useful within a discussion of Whiteread's work.

Firstly, there is the deferred 'referent', the absent thing which requires us to use a word to suggest it. Secondly, there is the retroactive deferral of meaning in any succession of two or more signs, whereby each sign (or word, to think linguistically) retains the 'ghosts' of its predecessors and is reliant on these traces for its meaning, just as it modifies retrospectively the meaning of the words it succeeds. Thirdly, there's the difference between words which is reliant on the gaps between them. Rather than being of no consequence, effectively absent in the sense of *not there*, these gaps are absent in the sense of *there*: this word is not that word by virtue of this 'ground of zero', and indeed the page itself.

Furthermore, this difference, deferral – *différance* – is the very grounds for language, both for written language (which for Saussure as well as many other philosophers, linguists and semioticians has been seen as a sort of lurid charlatan to the pure and natural form of spoken language) and, crucially, for speech itself. Even speech relies for its meaning on the play of differences between sounds (that one sound means one thing only by virtue of its difference from another sound, as opposed to any intrinsic quality of the sound which would link it in any meaningful way to the thing referred to). Rather than see writing as a mere 'external' representation of 'internal' speech[4] as Saussure does, Derrida insists that speech itself, in its reliance on difference, bears within itself a *propensity,* shall we say, to writing, what Derrida calls 'arche-writing', and which for him constitutes the (non) originary trace. Since the full extent of Derrida's complicated argument occupies a large part of *Of Grammatology*, and my focus here is, specifically, Rachel Whiteread's art, I can only refer you to Derrida's work for a fuller exposition.

At base, however, let's say that everything that is written – is made *concrete* – everything even that is said – signs that are wholly ephemeral – must fail to say other things in order for the statement to hold meaning. Yet what is written or said simultaneously relies for its meaning on this infinite and infinitely regressing web of language, which is assumed but yet must also be forgotten. To acknowledge every thread, every impulse would not only be impossible, but even if it were, would reduce meaning per se to the meaningless. Speaking of Foucault's *History of Madness*, Derrida insists that the repression of madness, as perceived by Foucault, from the madness/reason couplet can not be deemed in any way to have been a sort of prejudiced *choice* so much as having been a *necessity* when it comes to the formation of reason. This is not to say this repression should itself be repressed. It is a necessary forgetting, but the remembrance of it has formed Derrida's ongoing project.

It is this double bind which, perhaps more than any other aspect, makes Derrida's project so nearly impenetrable. That the split is *internal* to meaning is often conveniently overlooked by deconstruction's commentators. It is not simply the case that reason/madness (a dichotomy intimately linked with those other foundational dichotomies presence/absence, male/female, mind/body) divided from each other in the making of reason, and not only that each remains embedded in the other as a trace of the other, but that the split itself, as it were, constituted itself internally. This is far better explained by Derrida than myself, for fairly obvious reasons:

> The Decision, through a single act, links and separates reason and madness, and it must be understood at once both as the original act of an order, a fiat, a decree, and as a schism, a caesura, a separation, a dissection. I would prefer *dissension*, to underline that in question is a self-dividing action, a cleavage and torment interior to meaning *in general*, interior to logos in general, a division within the very act of *sentire*. As always, the dissension is internal. The exterior (is) the interior, is the fission that produces and divides it.[5]

This passage will form the basis of a closer look at the question of the worried line that both links and separates absence and presence in Whiteread's work and which comes close to being explicit in *Wall*: '*the dissension is internal. The exterior (is) the interior, is the fission that produces and divides it.*'

The first question when it comes to *Wall* is the question of where exactly the piece is, as it were, in this piece. The 'artwork' is called *Wall* (its full title is of course *Untitled (Wall)*, but given that Whiteread uses this device for her titles so frequently – an interesting decision in itself – the bracketed terms tend to be those commonly thought of as titles), yet the artwork comprises the wall, the cast of the wall, and

the space between. This suggests that all three of these 'elements' together constitute the 'wall'. It is as if the object (the wall) or at the very least the word 'wall' as
used for the title, is constituted *itself* by the split or space between *it* and *what it is
not*: an internal dissension indeed.

It is not simply the case that interior and exterior are reversed in Whiteread's
work, nor that in reversing them they are both called to mind at once. Yet neither
is it only the case that the interior implies the exterior through its indexical relationship to it. Rather the cast shifts from being simply an *index* for the absent object
to being both an index and a *signifier*. Where Whiteread calls the cast of a house
House, for example, she is not only (if at all) implying a sort of ironic melancholy
for the house that was, nor is she only recalling the absent house by naming the
cast as its (indexical) sign. It is both the absent house *and* the work called *House* that
together constitute the house as sign per se. *Wall*, as we shall see, makes this shift
between index and signifier explicit, a sliding sign system which comes closer to
C.S. Peirce's understanding of semiotics than Saussure's more rigid system.[6]   77

I have touched already on the importance of the indexical relationship
between mould and cast, and the way in which the knowledge of this intimacy in
Wall disturbs the sense of distance between the two elements as you walk between
them. For Whiteread the casting process itself is crucial: she is renowned for the
level of expertise she has in this area and conversations with people who make castings for a living (who also, oddly, number amongst my friends) confirm that some
of her work is almost impossible to make. Now if ever an artist before Whiteread
has worked so thoughtfully with both the making processes and concepts of mould
and cast as art (as opposed to as a process within the compound arts), it is Marcel
Duchamp. This is not an arbitrary comparison or a futile aside.

Works such as *Coin de chasteté*, 1954, which collides cast and mould into one
suggestive piece; *Feuille de vigne femelle (Female Fig Leaf)*, 1950, and *Objet-Dard
(Dart-Object)*, 1951, are all works which explore the cast-mould relationship. In
Duchamp's case this relation is often explicitly in relation to sexuality. Obviously
this is no random association: the penis/vagina, male/female, seen/not-seen,
light/dark chain of associations is the *very model* for phallogocentrism, absence and

presence and the hierarchies that have pertained to them.[7] Duchamp's interest in the relation between cast and mould goes much further than this straightforward binarism. In his *Boîte-en-valise* project of 1935–41, in which he made carrying cases full of miniatures of his most important (or at least more well-known) works, the strange bifurcations of the cast-mould relationship came in to play. For example, he had to hand-sculpt a miniature urinal in order to cast multiples from it, which was based in turn on the earlier urinal *Fountain, 1917.* This readymade, of course, had been a mass-produced object originally – one presumes – cast itself from a mould cast from a sculpted object.

Duchamp's fascination with this relationship is perhaps most apparent in his concept of *infra mince*. This word could very loosely be translated as 'ultra-thin', although rather than choosing the term *ultra mince, infra mince* implies a thinness that is below the range which can be perceived by the human (as in *infrared*). The term first appeared in a special edition of *View* magazine, published in 1945, for which Duchamp had designed the covers. The full set of Duchamp's notes on *infra mince* – 43 scraps of paper, envelopes, hotel notepaper, in total – were only repro-duced posthumously, in 1980, by his step-son Paul Matisse.[8]

Infra mince is always an adjective, Duchamp says, never a noun,[9] and there are many instances given, some more coherent than others. I will give here only a few: 'When the tobacco smoke smells also of the mouth which exhales it, the 2 odours marry by *infra mince* (olfactory *infra mince*)'[10]; 'Allegory (in general) is an application of the *infra mince*'[11] and, the example I want to focus on in relation to Whiteread's work, 'the difference between 2 mass-produced objects from the same mould...when the maximum precision is obtained'. Ades, Cox, Hopkins have pointed out that: 'What it [*infra mince*] aims to isolate is a kind of displacement that bears a trace with-out necessarily being "indexical"...a kind of interface or state of being "in between"', and also that 'Infra-thin then points to a condition of liminality, that is, something on the threshold (between inside and outside, for example)...a gap or shift that is vir-tually imperceptible but absolute'.[12] I take all this to be the case, yet I would like to think that *infra mince,* or at least Duchamp's intentions in formulating the concept, might be pinned down, if not mathematically, at least a little more precisely.

What *is* 'the difference between 2 mass-produced objects from the same mould...when the maximum precision is obtained'? Certainly maximum precision can never be infinite precision – so does Duchamp merely refer to the inevitable imprecision tolerated in the making process? In which case the answer might be: a millimetre or two. But then if it's only this, why bother to specify the maximum precision at all? Why not just ask what the differences between two casts are?

Rather I think there is more going on here. I would like to take the maximum precision to approximate infinite precision. In short, say that the casts are identical to each other. Still, they are not the same object. They are two distinct objects with exactly matching physical properties, both with the same indexical relation to the same object and yet not bearing an indexical relationship to each other, except via a third party.

These two objects differ in one simple physical and one dare I say it metaphysical way. Firstly, these two objects cannot occupy the same space at the same time. They can exist in the same space at a different time or the same time in a different space. There must either be a temporal or spatial difference; it doesn't matter which; and given this temporal/spatial difference or deferral, one might be perceived as representing or standing in for the other. Secondly, the only difference between them is that there is a difference between them. It cannot be seen, perceived, described, except by the laying of one next to the other. One simply is not the other. Given a deferral then (in time or space) one of these casts might feasibly be seen as a 'sign' for the other and yet, at the same time, both act as an indexical 'sign' for the mould. In this sense the casts, as signs for the mould, are interchangeable or, indeed, repeatable.

To return to *Wall*, it is worth noting that the most basic building block is the brick, and it is indeed a brick wall (rather than, for example, a plasterboard wall) that Whiteread has cast. Not only are words often colloquially referred to as the 'building blocks' of language, but architecture's passion for linguistics has often predicated architecture 'as a language'. The term is debatable. Yet it is true that architecture does have a certain set of repeatable elements, both in terms of classical architectural components – the column, the pediment etc. – and, on a more practical note, but one which *does* affect how architecture is designed, the repeat-able element of the standardized industrial component which is both easier to work with and more cost effective. Architects such as Charles Eames have made a virtue out of such components and maverick architects from Mannerism (Michaelangelo) to Po-Mo (James Stirling) have exploited the notion of the repeatable element in order to disrupt or subvert that same language.

For Derrida, a word's functioning *as* a word stems from its 'iterability', its abil-ity to be repeated, whilst at the same time never being the same word twice. Without this, a sound uttered in the moment whilst pointing to an object holds meaning only for that moment – in effect therefore it holds no meaning. For a sound to become a word – to enter into language – it must be repeated in connec-tion with a given object or referent. From then on it can be used in the absence of the referent and hold meaning: become a word. Indeed, to become a word, a signi-fier, it must necessarily displace or modify its referent.[13] The fact then that Duchamp's idealized cast is one of two casts referring indexically to the same mould points up the *iterable* nature of the cast. The very virtue of a mould is that it can produce numerous casts: multiples. The whole concept of mass-manufacture is based on this fact and the idea of the 'limited edition' artwork[14] only serves to highlight the need the art world has to remain wedded to the concept of the origi-nal as commodity, a notion which Duchamp of course consistently exposed in his display of ready-mades and in particular *Fountain* (which was signed R. Mutt, fur-ther muddying the waters of 'authorship').

Rosalind Krauss has discussed in depth Duchamp's complex relationship to the index, as well as the related notions of the 'original' and what she sees as its repressed partner-term, 'repetition'.[15] *With my Tongue in my Cheek*, 1959, as Krauss has noted, collides two sign systems: the index (the cast, indeed, of Duchamp's own cheek – with his tongue in it), and the icon (the cast is over-laid onto a line draw-ing of Duchamp's profile and eye). Rather than re-iterate these discussions I will only refer you to Krauss's essay, but in light of her concerns it is important to note too her observations on Surrealist photography.[16] In 'tricks' such as double expo-sure, solarization and the Rayogram (photogram), this photography, according to

Krauss, admits its status as sign (as sign indexically related to its referent). This is an internal doubling, or an internal splitting, dependent on your viewpoint, doubling – repeatability – being the flip-side of splitting since the moment a *thing* (for want of a better term) is doubled, it also admits of its fractured nature. (Both Krauss and Derrida agree on this point, not to mention Jacques Lacan).

Are Duchamp's two 'perfect' casts, then, the sign of the mould *doubled*, but also the single sign *split internally* to expose its own nature as sign? Is it by virtue of being repeated that they move beyond the status of index and onto that of signifier? So that where an instance of *infra mince* such as the tobacco/mouth relationship might lead us to believe that Duchamp's term refers only to an indexical relation, the mould/cast example, as well as the allegory (a leading to one thing via a decodable other thing, and which also verges beyond index and sign to symbol) suggests an engagement with the whole gamut of sign types, the entire range of C.S. Peirce's sliding system, and hence with the very process of language formation in which the sign's iterable nature is exposed through doubling/internal dissension.

Returning to Derrida's challenge to Foucault's complaint at the repression of madness, on the split between reason and madness being internal to the very formation of reason:

> Language being the break with madness, it adheres more thoroughly to its essence and vocation, makes a cleaner break with madness, if it pits itself against madness more freely and gets closer and closer to it: to the point of being separated from it only by the "transparent sheet"...that is, by itself – for this diaphaneity is nothing other than the language, meaning, possibility, and elementary discretion of a nothing that neutralizes everything.[17]

It would be wilfully perverse to avoid what are, at least, the metaphorical similarities between this 'transparent sheet' or 'elementary discretion' ('discretion' understood in the sense of a breaking into discrete elements but also perhaps in the sense of being discreet: quietly done, hidden, secretive even) and Duchamp's notion of *infra mince* (which in being 'infra' would also be, to the human eye, transparent). So that while it would be absurd to suggest that we could lay upon Duchamp a non word which was first coined twenty or so years after his death, (though he did claim to be fifty years ahead of his time) I would suggest that *infra mince* and *différance* have more than a few things in common, not the least of which being their status as neologisms and their nebulous nature as concepts.[18] In pre-structuralist and (dare I say it) pre-poststructuralist times, it seems Duchamp may have been edging around a somewhat hazy understanding of the issues that Derrida and his contemporaries would go on to (not) define: a sort of loosely intuited proto-*différance*. To return then to the matter at hand: the strangely expanded yet infinitely thin space in *Wall* (an embodiment or metaphor for this elementary discretion, this transparent sheet that lies between and binds together absence and presence and which lies at the very core of the condition of language). While I would not be so naïve as to state definitively that *Wall* materializes *différance* (and may even dematerialize it) I don't think I would be committing any deep theoretical sin to say that the infinitely thin gap here expressed might be described as *infra mince*.

Except of course that my formulation of *infra mince* in this case differs significantly from Duchamp's (as expressed in his cast-cast example). The relationship here is *not* between cast and cast, but between cast and mould. Given my attempt at rigour here, and my wish to move beyond metaphor – surely the critic's true vice – I admit this seems a sophist shift of thought. Furthermore, in Whiteread's work generally, the 'iterable' cast is undermined by the fact that, in almost all of her works, the original mould (the object) is actually destroyed in the making process. Is *House*, for example, iterable? Absolutely not, since the house had to be demolished in order to make *House* (its imminent demolition in fact being the very basis for Whiteread's decision to cast it).

We return once more to the unique nature of *Wall* within Whiteread's oeuvre. Here, as with *Monument*, the mould not only remains intact (and hence could feasibly be cast again and again) but is an integral part of the work. So I might, perhaps, have better described as *infra mince* the relationship between the cast of the wall and a further (potential, identical) cast of the wall. Yet *infra mince* as a concept is hazy at best, haphazard at worst. Perhaps, then, the level of precision attempted here is something of a mirage. The continued existence of the mould in *Wall* at least alludes to the potential for repetition and hence the potential – and elusive – relationship between them. Its difference in this respect from the rest of her oeuvre is also, then, what makes it a key (in the sense of code rather than exemplar) to that oeuvre. If *Wall* highlights the potential for iterability, it does it all the more to pinpoint the loss of continuity that occurs in the face of destruction, and the creation of the sign. This destruction, for Whiteread, is variously the destruction of ethics, of vernacular traditions, of ways of life and of life itself, and is crucial to the sense of loss that pervades her work, and which, in *Wall*, is present by its absence.

The relationship in *Wall* between cast and mould is not, then, strictly *infra mince* in the specific sense of Duchamp's example. Yet neither is there a straightforward relationship between the original object and the cast (or copy) of it. As I've noted, the *entire piece* is called *Wall*. One might say that not only is the cast here an indexical sign for the gallery wall, but the piece as a whole with its separation between mould/cast suggests an internal split or dissension which constitutes the 'wall' (with all its iterable brick-words) as language, and exposes the very nature of language formation.

One further observation before asking, finally, what *Wall* might have to say about the entirety of Whiteread's oeuvre. The 'gap' in *Wall* is, approximately, 'human' sized. Whilst this harks back, perhaps unintentionally, to Le Corbusier's design system (as in the monastery of La Tourette) based around human dimensions, it seems crucial to me that Whiteread places the human body *inside the split*, into the moment of *différance* and so at the heart of language formation. While this serves to drag the work (and indeed critics of the work such as myself) out of the mire of abstract theory and back into the traffic of the human body, perhaps it also recalls the origins of language in the human body – the larynx, the lips, the voice, in terms of speech, or the writing hand and seeing eyes in terms of written language. Given that according to Derrida, as we have seen, the very possibility of speech depends on the fundamental differences embedded within it, and that the written word is embedded as much in the spoken word as the spoken is in the written, this would not be an inappropriate comparison. The permutations are endless and, given that we are in any case assigning possible 'meanings' or at least 'alignments' to an artwork which makes no explicit claims to be doing any of the above, we may well be moving in futile circles. At the very least all of this opens up numerous if spurious insights into the layers of (possible and potential) meaning in Whiteread's work. In any case it may well be that Whiteread's work, which often seems so silent as to be mute, in fact speaks in many tongues.

If, as I have suggested, *Wall* is in many ways a *key* for Whiteread's work in general, then what are we to make of works such as *Ghost*? Given that what is fundamental to these works, as I hope I have shown, are the walls themselves, shouldn't we focus not on the void-made-solid, which is the space of the room, but on the walls stripped away to reveal the space of the room? For a good few inches around the work – the width of the brick, breezeblock or timber framework – there is, retained and invisible, the ghost of the old framing structure. This is literally the closest you can ever get to a 'room' without being inside it. Even gawping through a window like a Peeping Tom wouldn't get you so close as this wall-less solidified space. (Being unhelpful in this respect, perhaps the windows are 'blanked out' for a reason). While attention has been lavished on the ghost that is the absent living room (or house, or book, etc.), the ghost of the wall in such works has often been forgotten, and perhaps it is the absence of this wall that makes them so strange to the eye. *Ghost* is not only the ghost of the room that it is a cast of, but the ghost of its framing structure, its walls. In an opposite sense to *Wall* then, *Ghost* reveals the traces left by the workings of language internal to language itself. If *Ghost* rather coyly exposes its sensitive skin, the underbelly of language, *Wall* has no such inhibitions. The infinitely thin gap, on either side of which the index and its referent have slid apart, embodies the internal dissension that constitutes the signifier. Eliding any rigid distinction of signs into semiotic categories, *Wall* reveals the slippery shifts within the broken heart of language.

CHAPTER 4

MOVING ON

MELANIE MARIÑO

A maze is a house built purposely to confuse men; its architecture,
prodigal in symmetries, is made to serve that purpose. In the palace
that I imperfectly explored, the architecture had no purpose. There
were corridors that led nowhere, unreachably high windows, grandly
dramatic doors that opened onto monklike cells or empty shafts, incred-
ible upside-down staircases with upside-down treads or balustrades.

Jorge Luis Borges

This palace is set within the Borgesian fable, 'The Immortal', where it encircles a
small plaza in the City of the Immortals. The prodigious irrationality of its architecture recalls to the narrator 'the body of a tiger or a bull pullulating with teeth,
organs, and heads monstrously yoked together yet hating each other.'[1] This perverse after-image unfolds the imagination of a repellent impossibility. But the structure of that fiction also inducts the reader into the transient incongruities of memory, which braid past and future into an infinite and circular labyrinth.

Might this agile refutation of succession defer the pastness of history, refer to
art's end? The question is posed by Rachel Whiteread's art, whose intermingling of
real places and fictional fragments shadows the debates of the 1960s and 1970s.
Inhabiting the gap between sculpture and architecture, Whiteread's 'invented
spaces' insist on the very boundaries they refuse to delimit, for in her proposition,
the status of both mediums is inexact. Indeed, the condition of these works might
be characterized as ghostly in their form – they recast minimalism's stolid, industrial construction as sepulchral trace – and in their logic – they elaborate the subsequent generation's critique of minimalism through the dialectic of the afterlife.[2]

27   *Ghost* 1990, plaster on steel frame,
269 x 356 x 318cm (106 x 140 x 125in)

Whiteread's work was widely introduced to the American public in 1994 with
The Museum of Modern Art's exhibition, 'Sense and Sensibility: Women Artists
and Minimalism in the Nineties'.[3] That debut featured the aptly titled *Ghost*, 1990
(27), which inaugurated the artist's turn from casts of found domestic furniture
(such as mattresses, bathtubs, closets, sinks, and tables) to more ostensibly architectural projects (including *House*, *Water Tower*, and *Monument*, as well as *Holocaust
Memorial* in Vienna). Cast from the parlour room of an abandoned late Victorian
terrace house at 486 Archway Road, North London, *Ghost* stood like a dingy white
monument that reworked the unitary and serial forms of minimalism – for
instance, the poplar, steel, and plexiglass boxes of Donald Judd, Tony Smith, and
Anne Truitt – into an opaque index of the modest dwellings in which Whiteread
was raised. Supported by a steel frame, the monolith is pieced together from wide,
horizontal plaster block casts (whose depth spans no more than five inches) of the
room's stripped, sectioned, and smeared walls. *Ghost* inverts that interior lining,
moulding the outline of the door at the rear, the window at the side, the fireplace at
the front along with the residual imprints of wallpaper and soot into exterior façade.

87

At times, these torsions induce the oppressive sensation of claustrophobia.
The ceiling is open, but the viewer is barred from entering the room's interior.
Nevertheless, cracks in the walls allow us to peer into the hollow structure,
where we glimpse its metal skeleton and numbered panels. As in much
of Whiteread's work, the entombed container solicits comparison with the
funerary – the artist once worked at the Highgate Cemetery in North London
and frequented the Egyptian galleries at the British Museum. Whiteread explained,
'I had an idea of mummifying the sense of silence in the room.'[4] She creates,
one might say, that paradoxical 'image that produces Death while trying to
preserve life.'[5]

THE MINIMALIST BODY

Whiteread's shift in emphasis from domestic objects to architectural structures was
motivated by the ambition to de-literalize the former's connection to the body. The
artist once observed, 'I use furniture as a metaphor for human beings.'[6] Where the

beds, for instance, slump like bodies against walls, mutating into the shape of tongues, lips and folds, the casts of architectural structures and their parts, such as corners, floors, and stairs, do not represent surrogate bodies as much as they map abstract forms. Yet, the bodily analogy persists. For the artist continued to conceive of buildings as organic: 'I think of houses in terms of skeletons, the plumbing and electricity as nerves and blood vessels.'[7]

Of course, nothing could be more anathema to the rigorous abstraction of minimalism than anthropomorphism. Deploying non-relational shapes (as explored by the 1965 exhibition 'Shape and Structure') in tandem with the serial ordering of 'one thing after another' (for instance in Donald Judd's rows of galvanized iron cubes or Carl Andre's metal plates), minimal art refused to compose meaning as something behind the surface and inside the artist: repudiating the drama of the personal, the dimension of the subjective, its structures pressed outward, toward the surface, and beyond, toward the public here and now of perception.[8] As Frank Stella put it, 'what you see is what you see'.[9]

It might be objected that here, too, as Michael Fried intuited, the human body remains central.[10] Displacing the privilege accorded to the artist as the originator of a work's formal relationships, perception was re-sited within the viewer's grip so that 'one is more aware than before that he himself is establishing relationships as he apprehends the object from various conditions and under varying conditions of light and spatial context.'[11] Often, minimalism's non-hierarchical, multi-planed, geometrical constructions would move and bend at different angles, consistently shifting balance according to one's point of view. Indeed, it is the temporal movement of the body around the object, through its site, that completes the experience of '[an] equivalence between the orientation of the visual field and the awareness of one's own body as the potentiality of that field.'[12]

All of this translated, often quite consciously, the language of phenomenology. Published in English in 1962, Maurice Merleau-Ponty's *Phenomenology of Perception* offered an entire generation of artists the terms for a reorientation of vision around the viewer's lived corporeity: 'Our own body is in the world as the heart is in the organism: it keeps the visible spectacle constantly alive, it breathes life into it, and sustains it inwardly, and with it forms a system.'[13] Merleau-Ponty outlined the compound of body and world as a topology of changing perspectives. He writes, 'The inner horizon of an object cannot become an object without the surrounding objects becoming a horizon.' Subtending the extension of one view into another, vision becomes 'an act with two facets.'[14]

This doubling draws a relation of reciprocity, even identity, between the seer and seen. 'Since vision is a palpation with the look,' Merleau-Ponty elaborates in *The Visible and the Invisible*, 'as soon as I see, it is necessary that the vision....be doubled with a complementary vision or with another vision: myself seen from without, such as another would see me, installed in the midst of the visible.'[15] In the final chapter, the philosopher examines this twinning not as a splitting but as the chiasmatic crossing of the body's seeing and visible aspects: 'We say therefore that our body is a being of two leaves, from one side a thing among things and otherwise what sees them and touches them', he repeats, 'it unites these two properties within itself, and its double belongingness to the order of the "object" and to the order of the "subject"....teaches us that each calls for the other.'[16]

To imagine the passage of one into the other, we are asked to picture not two halves but rather an obverse and reverse. In his working notes to *The Visible*, Merleau-Ponty abbreviates this spatiality through the image of the finger of a glove turned inside out: within the philosopher's work, it is perhaps this lapidary figure of reversibility that draws us closest to the heart of Whiteread's casts. Coiling spatial metaphor into dynamic movement, he clarified, 'the only place where the negative would really be is the "fold", the application of the inside and the outside to one another, the turning point.' Whiteread's inverted structures give form to that archetype of negative presence: 'The end of the finger of the glove is nothingness – but a nothingness one can turn over, and where then one sees things.'[17]

UNMAKING SCULPTURE/UNBUILDING ARCHITECTURE

Quite blatantly, Whiteread herself spelled out a specific, critical connection to the codified discourse of minimal art. *Untitled (One Hundred Spaces)*, to cite the most

89

obvious example, multiplied Bruce Nauman's *A Cast of the Space under My Chair* (1965–68) into a hundred multi-colour translucent resin replicas, according her work an immediate authority, while prompting some critics to protest, 'You're just making Naumans.'[18] For Nauman, negative space involved 'thinking about the underside and backside of things.'[19] Whiteread's inversions employ the negative cast to harden inaccessible spaces inside, underneath, and between objects and spaces into mass, whose lightness also recall Eva Hesse's seemingly weightless fibreglass and resin extrusions (for instance, *Repetition Nineteen III*, 1968, or *Accretion,* 1969).[20]

Subsumed in its day under the banner of 'Anti Form' and 'Process Art', the works of Nauman and Hesse fragmented minimalism's well-built, industrial objects, piling, hanging, and stacking impoverished materials like rubber, cheese-cloth and wood shavings to explore the properties of matter and literalize its capitulation to the pull of gravity. For Robert Smithson, the 'process' of art trans-lated an action of 'unmaking' – which he also allied with the laws of entropy.[21] In his essay 'Entropy and the New Monuments' Smithson referred to entropy's irre-versible propulsion toward disorder to draw a picture of a 'new kind of monumentality'.[22] He elaborates, 'They are not built for the ages, but rather against the ages. They are involved in a systematic reduction of time down to frac-tions of seconds, rather than representing the long spaces of centuries.'[23] Within Smithson's work 'the arrow of time', as entropy is also called, is at times conceived in terms of material degeneration ('time as decay') and at others, as static inertia ('this kind of time has little or no space, it is stationary and without movement, it is going nowhere').[24]

It was the second modality of entropy as 'motionless time' that Smithson explored in 'A Tour of the Monuments of Passaic', his quixotic journey through the desolate industrial landscape of New Jersey that bordered Passaic's polluted river. Published as an illustrated travelogue in the December 1967 issue of *Artforum*, the essay charted the artist's movement from the bridge linking Bergen and Passaic Counties through the construction site of an unfinished highway along the river and finally into the town centre. Eight images of the 'rotting industrial town' accompany a guidebook description of the suburb's 'zero panorama', whose banal and empty spaces exemplified the 'all-encompassing sameness' Smithson associated with entropy's energy drain. For Smithson, those places also adduce the time in which 'both past and future are placed into an objective present,'[25] generating the monuments he characterized as 'ruins in reverse, that is - all the new construction that would eventually be built.'[26]

Examples of such ruins abound in Smithson's writings: he illustrated an interview, 'Entropy Made Visible', with photographs of a construction pit in Central Park topped by precariously balanced fences and machines; a street shattered by an earthquake in Anchorage, Alaska; a row of houses abutting the site of a volcanic eruption. And in his own work, he enacted this entropic building with such architectural projects as *Partially Buried Woodshed*, 1970, for which he poured twenty loads of earth on an abandoned woodshed on Ohio's Kent State University campus, eventually cracking the shed's interior central beam.

This radical photographic and architectural disordering of monumental time partnered with another kind of dislocation. To his revision of construction as ruination, Smithson apposed a model of perception as corporeal disorientation. This is, for instance, the experience projected by Smithson toward the conclusion of the Passaic essay, 'One never knew what side of the mirror one was on.'[27] It also forms a principal theme in his *Spiral Jetty*, 1970. Confronted by the elegant serpentine geometry of mud, salt crystals, black rocks, and algae twisting across the northern end of Utah's Great Salt Lake, Smithson is literally precipitated beyond himself. 'On the slopes of Rozel Point I closed my eyes, and the sun burned crimson through the lids', he recounts, 'Between heat lightning and heat exhaustion the spiral curled into vaporization. I had the red heaves, while the sun vomited its corpuscular radiations.'[28] Sweeping through the different points of the compass – North, North by East, Northeast by North, and so on – a sequence from the Spiral Jetty film manouvres the sun's reflection into the Jetty's centre, whose 'dizzying spiral' withholds the 'assurance of geometry', deranging the coherence of perception: '*Et in Utah ego*. I was slipping out of myself again, dissolving into a unicellular beginning, trying to locate the nucleus at the end of the spiral.'[29]

Divested of coordinates, perception, like the 'rotary that enclosed itself',[30] is de-centred. But this de-centring – which, in many ways, retracted entropy's slide into the formlessness of the sublime, of the 'nothing further happening' – also accomplishes a re-siting. After all, there is a difference, as Smithson suggested, between the 'experience before the physical abyss' and that 'before the mapped version.'[31] It is that difference that remaps art as a 'back and forth thing' set within the grip of 'a process of ongoing relationships.'[32]

It was left to Richard Serra to most systematically pursue the logic of that process as a 'dialectic of walking and looking into the landscape.'[33] Around 1970, with works such as *Shift*, 1970–72, and *Sight Point*, 1971–75, Serra began to develop the experience of sculpture in terms of the peripatetic spectator's reading of tectonic form and its surrounding terrain: 'The placement of all structural elements in the open field draws the viewer's attention to the topography of the landscape as the landscape is walked.'[34] Those elements 'point to the indeterminacy of the landscape',[35] drawing into focus a shifting terrain, whose 'form remains ambiguous, indeterminable, unknowable as an entity.'[36]

Now and then, Serra appears to offer a geometric key to the reading of his works. For *Spin Out (for Robert Smithson)*, 1973, for instance, he relates the installation of three hot rolled steel plates onto the sloped planes of the garden of the Kröller-Müller Museum in the following way: 'The plates were laid out at twelve, four and eight o'clock in an elliptical valley, and the space in between them forms an isosceles triangle.'[37] The actual circumnavigation of this work, however, yields no such experience of geometry. Rather, the viewer – standing in the middle of the grass clearing – is pulled to both sides by the asymmetrically placed planes and simultaneously pushed forward onto the woody periphery by a half-concealed protrusion. Following the work's centrifugal dispersal, the spectator is propelled along and around its scattered cues, away from the location of any centre.

In this way, *Spin Out*'s topology functions like *Shift*. Initially conceived to maintain the mutual viewpoint of two people navigating the rise and fall of uneven farm land, *Shift* coordinates six concrete elevations as a network of moving perspectives that simultaneously 'suggest themselves as orthogonals within the terms of a perspective system of measurement', while disabling the fixed lines upon which Renaissance space depended: 'These steps relate to a continually shifting horizon, and as measurements, they are totally transitive: elevating, lowering, extending, foreshortening, contracting, compressing, and turning. The line as a visual element, per step, becomes a transitive verb.'[38] These actions turn on the passage of viewer through space. That is, they are generated by changes in bodily position that ascribe the sighting of the work's fluctuating horizon to the mutuality of spectator and site – Serra cast this transitivity in architectural terms, as a play of parallax.[39]

TOWARD ANARCHITECTURE

Smithson and Serra built their site works around a moving centre, elusive in its regress and even dissipative in its progress. For the generation that followed, this discontinuous movement would form the impossible ground of a new kind of architecture, of 'anarchitecture'. Coined by Matta-Clark, the term did not denote an opposition to architecture as such but rather an 'alternative attitude to buildings.'[40] Anarchitecture as title rather than practice also identified an informal association of artists organized in 1973, who convened in Richard Nonas's studio as well as restaurants and bars,[41] where its members improvised collaborative proposals concerned with 'metaphoric voids, gaps, leftover spaces, places that were not developed.'[42] For the group, these liminal spaces occupied the fringes of built architecture; neither within nor beyond architecture, they were significant for their 'reference to movement space'.[43]

In March 1974, the Anarchitecture group installed an exhibition anonymously at 112 Greene Street, an artist's space in New York's SoHo. Apart from the drawings of Nonas and Laurie Anderson and a photo-collage by Jene Highstein, the show comprised standardized black-and-white photographs, which were subsequently published as a two-page spread in the June issue of *Flash Art*. These doleful pictures circled repeatedly around the ruinous and the mundane, as though to frame the disjecta of everyday life – a double row of abandoned containers set in a field of overgrown weeds, annotated 'an old façade: packed and waiting'; receding views of a decrepit Classical pillar; the black pit of a hole in the

93

28 *Demolished* 1996, 4 of 12 duotone screenprints, 49 x 74.4cm (19¹/₄ x 29¹/₄in)

ground; and so on. Among these fragments, three images are peculiarly resonant: the debris of train wreckage partially buttressed by crumbling walls (*Anarchitecture: Train Bridge*); a type of disposable home floated on a river barge (*Anarchitecture: Home Moving*); and a partial view of the World Trade Center's twin towers, their vertical rise awkwardly truncated, framing an interstice of clouded sky (*Anarchitecture: The Space Between*).

The 'movement' in these stills follows the trajectory of obsolescence. These objects and spaces are not so much on the go as on the way out. *The Space Between*, to take the most unsettling example, was accompanied by a rough sketch of the two towers separated by the half-submerged shape of a rayed sun arced over a horizon line. Entitled 'The Perfect Structure', the schematic drawing crossed out both sky-scrapers with an 'X' and appended a scribbled mandate on the right margin: 'Erase all the buildings on a clear horizon'.[44] This figural obliteration opposed the newly dedicated towers' vertical encroachment on celestial space – the photograph's image of the negative space between the towers salvages the remainder of that infringement. More importantly, Matta-Clark's gesture of subversive redemption critiqued the abuses of social space distilled by the Center's construction – namely, the excessive concentration of (actual and symbolic) capital in Manhattan's Financial District and architecture's complicity with that economy of 'luxurious squandering', with destructive expenditure masked as productive accumulation.[45]

Such economic logic finds explicit visual expression in Whiteread's *Demolished* (1996) (28). Created around the same time as *House*, this series of twelve photo screenprints records the demolition of residential tower blocks in London's East End. Like Matta-Clark's anarchitectural project, Whiteread's documents produced a provisional materialist investigation of the 'space between'. Several terms bracket that space – for instance, utility, property, commerce – circumscribing a situational practice that reframed sculpture's tendency to aestheticize architecture, on one hand, and architecture's capitulation to commercial rationalization, on the other.

In this way, Whiteread's work reanimates Matta-Clark's earlier interventions, which resisted the reduction of architecture to building ('architecture could be used to symbolize all the hard-shelled cultural reality') and reworked anarchitecture as

29 *Untitled (Stairs)* 2001, mixed media, 375 x 550 x 220cm (147 x 217 x 87)

kinaesthetic process (as 'undoing' or 'unbuilding').[46] In his early work this 'unbuilding' typically involved the removal of parts of condemned properties, an incision into architectural refuse that reshaped the spatial interaction of art and architecture. Consider, for example, *Bronx Floors*, 1972–73. For this series, Matta-Clark, assisted by Manfred Hecht, illegally cut geometrical sections out of the floors and walls of abandoned buildings in the Bronx.[47] Exhibited at 112 Greene Street, the series consisted of grouped views of the cavities, shot from vertiginous perspectives that refused to coalesce into a determinate whole, carving out a visual experience of a warped architectural crossing. The exhibition also included the actual building extractions, paired with photographic records of the original sites of removal.[48] Several of those extractions, including *Bronx Floors: Floor Above, Ceiling Below*, appeared to rotate the floor into the vertical extension of a sculptural object. This quite literal elevation, however, only partially assumed the identity of sculpture. Awkwardly tilted on its side, the 'sandwich' displayed an anonymous Bronx floor – with the peeled brown plaster and tawdry linoleum patterns of its horizontal board, along with thick wooden joists and strips of a ceiling section. The layered chunk lay open for the viewer's dissection, soliciting a reading of its previous function (as an architectural remnant) as well as the ground it inhabited (as a sculptural object). Extending the minimalist analysis of how a work sits on the floor, it also impelled the scrutiny of the floor's physical structure, inviting a comparison of the architectural foundations of sculpture with the sculptural conditions of architecture.

But it was another, now canonical, work that most aggressively forced that contrast. On 322 Humphrey Street in Englewood, New Jersey, an abandoned two-storey frame house slated for demolition was spliced open to create the bluntly titled *Splitting*, 1974. Extant only in photographic form today, the house appears literally sawed in half. Two vertical lines slice through the structure's central axis, substituting for floors, walls, stairs, and ceiling an empty sliver of sky not unlike that bracketed by *The Space Between*. Voided of its mid-section, the house rocks back toward the inclined ground behind it, prying the gash into a wedge that widens as it approached the cleaved roof.[49]

A kind of 'threshole' Matta-Clark situated between 'underground and sky', *Splitting* cut through the division between inside and outside, sculpture and architecture, building and landscape. If in works like *Bronx Floors*, Matta-Clark projected the space of architecture (the original sites) into the place of sculpture (the gallery) as so many optical disjunctions, *Splitting* produced those previously distinct experiences simultaneously, through the course of the viewer's actual bodily movement through the site. Like Smithson before him, who supplemented the 'Monuments' essay with actual guided tours of Passaic's ruins,[50] Matta-Clark also chartered a tour bus to take visitors from SoHo to the Englewood house.

While working on the Englewood home, Matta-Clark effused, 'The realization of motion in a static structure was exhilarating.'[51] For others, the effect was even more extreme: the movement through tilted stairs and doorways into the void generated, it appeared, the effect of 'abyss'. Alice Aycock recalled, 'As you'd go further up, you'd have to keep crossing the crack. It kept widening as you made your way up...by the time you got to the top the crack was one or two feet wide. You really had to jump it. You sensed the abyss in a kinaesthetic and psychological way.'[52]

Several critics have compared Matta-Clark's work to Whiteread's *House*. Isolated behind a remnant fence on an empty grass turf, the bunker-like hulk turned the original rooms inside out, casting the interior's walls, doors, and windows as a series of interlocked volumes that placed visitors outside the very interior view they could not escape. For some, the sudden intrusion of the dysfunctional ghost house on the street marred the neighbourhood's appearance – its neighbours, one journalist reported, 'only want to see the back of it – so to speak.'[53] But perhaps what was most disturbing was less this view than the psycho-social effects its perception provoked. Like Matta-Clark's splitting of the security of the middle-class suburban American home, Whiteread's *House* filtered the groundlessness of architecture through the disintegration of domestic and social spaces, inducing an uncanny misrecognition.

MOVING ON: ROOMS, FLOORS, AND STAIRS

In her recent series of apartment rooms, staircases (29), and floors, Whiteread continued to develop the ways 'the body in destination'[54] might reframe such 'abandoned boundary places', that is, 'the forced-open places, the not-yet-existent places, the unseen because unknown places; the pariah places and objects.'[55] Whiteread's works are cast from an empty building that would become the artist's studio and apartment in Bethnal Green, East London. Formerly a Baptist church before it became a synagogue in the 1900s, the building was rebuilt in the mid-1950s following its bombing in 1941, and had since assumed different functions, first as a plywood warehouse and then as a textile factory.[56] Comprised of two apartments, which formed the living spaces of the rabbi and the caretaker, the empty structure also possessed three concrete staircases, with one leading unexpectedly into a large basement.

Untitled (Basement), 2001 (30), is the negative incarnation of this staircase. The artist's first staircase work, the massive structure is cast in a plasticized plaster that crosses the surface qualities of plaster with the tougher properties of fibreglass, encasing the whole in a blank, chalky surface that invokes the look of industrial process. Turned precariously on its side, the terraced form lies down on the floor like a body laid to rest. (Typically called a 'coffin stair', the dimensions of such staircases were determined by the space needed to transport a coffin lifted by three men on each side.) Although impressed with the dark marks of passage, the stairs now flip to one side, as though to formalize their fall into disuse – they will no longer take us up or down. Nevertheless, the experience of the fallen object is given through its architectural surround, to be navigated bodily, successively, on the ground and through the floor.

Untitled (Cast Iron Floor), 2001 (31), discloses a parallel concern with passage. Cast from the entrance hall to the synagogue, this metal rendition of the initial plaster cast inverts the floor's original texture so that, for instance, the mortared ridges would extrude rather than withdraw into the planar surface. While they recall Andre's hard zinc and magnesium tiles, the raised black field of the grid is patinated and waxed to register the alterations wrought by the viewer's interaction with the object. The viewer's movement across its surface – repeated again and again – softens the raised lines into a sheen that would expose the floor's original notching. Like *Untitled (Basement)*, this cast also rotates space into the sequence of bodily tra-

30 *Untitled (Basement)* 2001, mixed media, 325 x 658 x 367cm (128 x 259 x 145in)

31 *Untitled (Cast Iron Floor)* 2001, cast iron and black patina, 99 units, overall dimensions 1 x 502 x 411cm ($^3/_8$ x 197$^3/_4$ x 161$^7/_8$in)

versal. But unlike that work, the floor retains its use as a thoroughfare, absorbing the marks of that movement, the better to diagram the newest chapter of its already sedimented history. As the artist explained, 'They are about walking over something, about what our presence actually does to a surface.'[57]

That history's complex temporality of disintegration (which erases the floor's relief pattern) and presence (which brings into view its previous outline) is restated by *Untitled (Apartment)*, 2000–01 (32), as a jagged spatial meander.[58] Cast in parts over a period of six months, Whiteread's reproduction of the synagogue's multi-roomed upstairs apartment unfastened its armature by fitting the white cubical sections loosely so that the walls were recreated as spaces, affording a view into narrow corridors, into inside panels and their remnant electrical joinery. Like the stairs that will lead nowhere, the apartment sits on the floor 'like a maze',[59] its neutral surfaces bearing the most minimal traces of wallpaper and paint.

The artist declared, 'We live in that kind of place', and she asked, 'how do we function physically within a place like that?'[60] The sense of constriction in archetypal modern flats – where small arm-span rooms and ill-considered walls tend to block movement – is plotted by corridors that lead into different planes in depth, their autonomous fragments cut off from one another. Shifting the body in and out of the asymmetrical grid, the work hinders the consecution of one place after another: 'You'll be able to walk around part of the piece, but then you'll have to back out, and go around the other way. So you'll never see the piece as a whole.'[61] The identity of the whole is replaced by a fractured architectural space, now organized as a futile rotary circulation whose divergences are left to the viewer to make sense of and connect in memory, over time.

A PHOTOGRAPHIC LOGIC

Such spatial discontinuities are akin to photography's own temporal halts. Stasis is critical to the photographic still, which 'embalms time'.[62] In their status as index, as physical traces of their referents, Whiteread's casts have often courted comparison with the photographic negative. Indeed, the artist has often described 'recording' as

32 *Untitled (Apartment)* 2000–01, plasticised plaster, wood and steel,
overall dimensions 282 x 1109 x 614cm (111 x 441 x 242in)

a principal theme of her work and discussed her recent series of rooms, floors, and stairs in terms of 'taking photographs or making prints of the space.'[63]

In the catalogue for the Guggenheim Museum's exhibition of *Untitled (Basement)* and *Untitled (Apartment)*, Whiteread also included a photo-essay, a compendium of fifty-one variously sized and formatted photographs that served, like the artist's wood models, hatched drawings and correction fluid photo-collages, as indices of her conceptual process. The images draw into focus now familiar preoccupations. Throughout, there are signs of waste and abandonment: unhinged doors propped against the wall of a council flat in Hackney, East London; a mound of firewood set before the blank window frames of a concrete building in Turkey; in Ireland, the grey stone façade of a gouged house bleeding into a craggy hill behind. The essay circles repeatedly around the zone in-between: the stream that ripples through a verdant gorge in the Rio Grande; a line of rock protruding from the light-dappled waters of Cinque Terre, Italy; the decline of narrow steps enframed by white walls. Often, these spaces are linked to images of anarchitecture, of splitting: in an open landscape, a mobile home is unexpectedly cleaved in half; a section of board is gingerly detached from its horizontal wall of cherry wood slats; a monumental rise of sandy stone cracked down the middle exposes a zone of shadow and splinters.

Like Whiteread's sculpture, these mundane pictures document places of loss, failure, and entropy, those objects and sites on the verge of extinction. But again like Whiteread's sculpture, these images have already entered into 'flat death', to borrow Roland Barthes's description of photography's leap, with the click of a shutter, to that zone outside language. But that condition, which we might also characterize as outside culture, would not preclude the medium's peculiar astonishment. This was, of course, the *punctum* or wound Barthes located in the anterior future of the photographic record, the paradoxical conflation of this-has-been with this-will-be. 'By giving me the absolute past of the pose (aorist), the photograph tells me death in the future.' He is horrified by this impossible equivalence, which presents: 'a catastrophe that has already occurred. Whether or not the subject is already dead, every photograph is this catastrophe.'[64]

This deathly matrix compels another consideration of Whiteread's architectural turn. For Barthes, the photograph functions as the modern antonym of the monument: 'Earlier societies managed so that memory, the substitute for life, was eternal and that at least the thing which spoke Death should be immortal: this was the Monument. But by making the (mortal) Photograph into the general and somehow natural witness of "what has been", modern society has renounced the Monument.'[65] How does Whiteread develop this a-monumental torsion of live image into 'flat death'?

The singularity of Whiteread's art derives from its adherence to its referents. Each work is a direct imprint of something unique and particular and as such disrupts perception's 'sensitivity for similarity'.[66] As views into the unseen and overlooked, Whiteread's structures pierce through the blind field of sameness that homogenizes our everyday lives. But their distinction also derives from their deathliness, their reference to real objects and places that have existed elsewhere. For Whiteread, the corpse of that referent is alive. For her works function as both archaeological document and mnemonic provocation, exhuming forgotten layers of history as they innovate new spaces for recollection.

AFTERLIFE

'The development of artworks', Adorno once wrote, 'is the afterlife of their immanent dynamic.'[67] This formulation pictures the afterlife as a belated historical development, as that which comes after to unfold a contradiction in art's inner logic. Doubling anticipation with memory, the afterlife encapsulates that elaboration as a moving on in the present. How do we read that afterlife in Whiteread's work?

As minimalism emphasized the viewer's bodily movement through sculpture's surrounding field, subsequent, post-minimal practices worked out of that relay between subject and space to redefine place as the enactment of a 'situation'. Within the practice of anarchitecture, to return to an earlier example, place was no longer centred by an architectural container so much as ejected to the fringe, and its demarcation was no longer dictated by the boundaries of form but rather released by locomotion. Significantly, such innovations refocused defunct social spaces – for

105

instance, the cast-offs of suburban confinement, of urban gentrification and blight – whose apprehension became a function of the viewer's motivation.

This is, of course, the dynamic resuscitated by Whiteread's work, whose differential triangulation of the sculptural, the architectural, and the photographic turn object, space, and viewer inside out. But if those inversions, as we have seen, drive our attention toward the quotidian structures of daily living, they also cultivate the perception of their hidden historical referents – for instance, the consequences of British imperialism, or Thatcherite politics in the 1980s; the trajectory of urban renewal in London and New York over the last two decades; the legacy of the Holocaust in Austria in the present. Those historical reminders, as we have also seen, form the obverse of literalist presence. Their pathos derives from the play of presence and absence, carving out the identity and possibility of contemporary aesthetic practice as a recuperation of what remains, as an injunction to look back as we move on, however spectrally, as ghosts.

CHAPTER 5

GOTHIC PUBLIC ART
AND THE FAILURES OF DEMOCRACY:
Reflections on *House*, Interpretation and the 'Political Unconscious'

ANGELA DIMITRAKAKI

Rachel Whiteread's *House* (33, 36), the impenetrable, life size cast of a Victorian house, is one of the most widely discussed art projects of the late twentieth century. For a large, open-air sculpture made out of concrete, it was also a remarkably short-lived one, standing its ground in east London's Grove Road from October 25, 1993 to January 11, 1994. That the work appeared and then promptly *disappeared* after merely three months in the international art capital of the 1990s, like a temporary, 'twilight-zone' disturbance in the force field of the public 'sphere', greatly augmented its impact and has since threatened to canonize it as an art historical myth.

Perhaps the most lamentable aspect of this myth is an implicit sedimentation of meaning, according to which *House* is seen as a typically scandalous incident in the context of the Brit Art ethics that ultimately defined the 1990s.[1] It should not be at all surprising then that an image of *House* decorates the cover of Richard Cork's recent anthology of his critical writings, largely focusing on the London scene. Cork opens with a discussion of *House*'s demolition, reminiscing about how, at the time, he had thought of this as a sign of Britain's 'rabid philistinism'.[2] Strangely, however, Cork goes on to say that 'against all the odds' the 1990s disproved his pessimism.[3] But if this was so, and the decade unfolded in such a way as to suggest that the troubling response to *House* was merely an aberration, a false alarm, and that things had indeed changed, the choice of this particular artwork as the cover image for a book dedicated to the 1990s makes little sense.

From another angle however, the choice seems ideal. True to its uncanny nature, the image of *House* disrupts the smooth, seamless narrative of optimism

33 *House* 1993. Full size cast.

which the reader encounters in Cork's text. You read about all the good things that happened in the 1990s but as soon as you close the book, there *it* is – in supremely ironic form, if one recalls Barthes's famous association of photography and death – a *photograph* of the thing that no longer exists and that was allegedly *not* a symptom of anything after all. There is, though, no need to look for the Barthesian punctum in this photograph.[4] In its particular context, the cover illustration itself has come to operate as the *punctum* of the book's tale: the disturbing detail, the 'prick' that may make one suspect that the aberration, the irregularity, may actually be playing a far more important role in how one understands the decade. In a certain sense then, that photograph of *House* reclaims the 1990s myth for the purposes of history.

In the transformation of a random sample of Victorian architecture into a piece of 'contemporary Gothic', (a genre that is, as is well known, 'no longer exclusively at home in medieval castles'[5]) *House* was of course neither aberration nor false alarm. *House* made a traditional London house look like a modernist cube which had undergone a terrifying mutation. But my nomination of the structure as gothic public art has less to do with the impression of hybridity its image conjured – a salient feature of postmodern architecture to which we are all more or less accustomed – and more to do with the responses invited by the gaps and cracks of its surfaces. The controversy that broke around this particular piece of sculpture, a structure turned inside out, suggested that *House* was relevant to a wider realm of intersecting debates, ranging from the meaning of public space in art (and vice versa) to the meaning of democracy, with the relationship between the two clearly being the most unsettling.

Ten years on the debates persist, and so does the memory. I belong to those who never had a first-hand experience of *House* in all its concrete physicality. And yet, while researching and teaching the history of this 'artwork', it became increasingly clear that I had what could be called an 'imaginary memory' of it. The contradiction within this phrase is purposefully invoked here to stand metonymically for the whole set of contradictions that *House* – or rather, its phantom-memory – evokes. In other words, I see Whiteread's project (and in that I also include the work's conceptualization and the debates that ensued around its erection and dem-

109

olition) as a nodal point which affords us the opportunity to enact a dialectical reading of the multiple threads – both discursive and material – that constitute the framework of the work's production and reception.

Providing a sustained analysis of these multiple threads lies beyond the scope of this essay, but it may in any case be an impossible task, given that *House* has been so extensively written about. Instead, my intention is to emphasize certain spatial paradigms and economies in a partial, but politically motivated, reading of this project, as well as of the construction of a 'contemporary' moment in art and culture – for which, I believe, *House* still holds a significance that has not yet been fully explained. In particular, I am interested in relating *House* to what Fredric Jameson has aptly named the 'political unconscious' of the culture that gave rise to it and which then proceeded to eliminate it.

Tentatively we could begin by saying that the political unconscious is a form of *haunting* (and let us not forget that haunting became a key term in analyses of *House*). The political unconscious permeates process and structure, and alludes to those repressed elements that nevertheless find their way into cultural forms, including art. The political unconscious is however historical. It is a hidden sign of the times, an invisible umbilical cord connecting reality and representation. To take a further step, the political unconscious allows and, simultaneously, enables us to question the loss of distinction between reality and representation. Difficult as it is to pin down the political unconscious of any given era and geography, or even offer a full definition of the concept, it is important to stress one of its more salient, operational characteristics. The political unconscious resides in the *object* as well as in the act and mode of *interpretation.*[6] One might be tempted to suggest that the political unconscious is enacted at the crossroads where the object and interpretation meet.

For the purposes of this essay, the appeal to the political unconscious aims, among other things, to dispel the illusion of the artwork's innocence. Despite the exaggerated (but also disaffected) white cube aesthetic of the structure, the walls of *House* were never a tabula rasa on which the 'public' from various walks of life could simply impose the burden of meaning. As far as the realm of 'action' is concerned (the privileged social space where decisions are made that is not however conflict-free), the choices made by the makers and destroyers of *House* could already be seen to 'reflect a fundamental dimension of our collective thinking and our collective fantasies about history and reality.'[7]

To give one example: *House* was always conceived by its makers – the artist and the commissioning agency, Artangel Trust – as a temporary construction. It was to be a sculpture with an expiry date. Yet its fate was ultimately realized by those in power (the local Council) who might never have perceived *House* as art in the first place. But what was it, in that cultural moment, that first made the conception (34) of such a 'temporary' sculpture possible in the minds of its ideological opponents and, then, licensed the act of destruction? (35) The question – let alone any possible answer it might receive – becomes more complicated if one moves away from what I have called above the 'realm of action', to consider the reactions of those *not* in power, those not able to make decisions about either the making or unmaking of a work of art (or non-work of art, according to some) that cost approximately £50,000 and that was erected in a public space. To the extent that such reactions were recorded, even outside the channels of the press that customarily 'mediates' public response, they appear to be divided. An ICA video recording a discussion among experts, and an edited volume entitled *House*, which appeared in 1995, closely after the demolition of the work, both offer ample evidence of such a split. What the videotaped discussion and the book documented was, first, the diverse discursive frameworks to which *House* lent itself and, secondly, the fault line running down the middle of 'public' opinion. But what did this division in public opinion mean? What did it convey to those with the power to ascribe meaning? Significantly, what this split suggests in the first instance is that the recovery of a political unconscious is a futile exercise. The political unconscious appears *not to be one*.

As John A. Walker argued retrospectively, 'what was unusual [*in the case of House*] was that opinions did not fall into familiar categories: here art world opinion versus those of the laypeople, because some locals liked and welcomed the sculpture while others detested it; opinion in the art world was similarly split.'[8]

34   *Study for 'House'* 1992–93, correction fluid on laser copy, 2 sheets,
60 x 42cm (23⁵/₈ x 16¹/₂in)

One may wonder of course what 'familiar categories' actually means in this case, since, when thinking about social divisions, a differentiation between 'the art world' and 'laypeople' is not the first distinction that comes to mind. Elsewhere, Walker writes:

> According to Lingwood [co-director of Artangel], Whiteread's House pro-
> voked 'a multiplicity of convictions, a host of different thoughts and
> responses' which it was not possible to explain in terms of old battle
> formations or partisan blocs of opinion, such as the art world versus
> the general public or the middle versus the working classes, 'because
> differences were always *within* identifiable groups of people, rather
> than *between* them.' He [Lingwood] concluded: 'House laid bare the
> limits of consensus. It did not expect to be ring-fenced from the con-
> tingencies of everyday life.'[9]

I find this illuminating. Here, not only the lack of consensus, but also the alleged dissolution of 'traditional' collective subjects, (say, the middle class and the working class), are elevated to the 'meaning' of House. Most importantly, the revelation of such ruptures is presented, and even celebrated, as a positive contribution made by the work. At the point however where such an overarching meaning is proposed we begin to get a glimpse of the political unconscious, which – contrary to what I claimed above – appears now *to be one*. Irrespective of whatever other 'meanings' may have been attributed to House by its multitude of 'publics' and individuals, the fact of differing views becomes the work's meaning par excellence. Moreover, in a sweeping move, the same fact is explicated as an overthrow of 'old battle formations' (for example 'the middle versus the working classes') as if there ever was a moment in history when a certain 'consciousness' could be seen to inhabit, transparently and unequivocally, the mind of each and every agent involved in class struggle (and the 'old battle formations'). Such a tenet can only be upheld if class struggle is misperceived in rather mechanistic terms (by the literal-minded), thus foreclosing a reading of class in terms of extremely complex social *relations*. Given that the postmodern thesis of this precise meaning, *the difference pointing to the demise of collective subjects*, has been argued to the point of exhaustion, in

35   The demolition of *House*

terms of either praise or lament, by theorists of the postmodern ranging from Baudrillard to Jameson, it is tempting to assume that this most facile of interpretations reveals something about the wider social and ideological experience of the interpreters.[10] What makes the dual invocation of the absence of consensus and the affirmation of difference trivial, but also troubling, as the specific artwork's ultimate 'message', is their frequent reiteration in recent cases of controversy over public art. Who doesn't remember Serra's *Tilted Arc*, 1981, to mention a well-known example, where the public inhabitation and use of public space was debated? In her essay 'Tilted Arc and the Uses of Democracy', Rosalyn Deutsche discussed the legal battle over the removal of Serra's sculpture from New York's Federal Plaza in 1989 (only five years before *House*) in precisely these terms. Her conclusion is that 'public space...is the uncertain social realm where, in the absence of an absolute foundation, the meaning of the people is simultaneously constituted and put at risk.'[11] This essay appears in a volume tellingly called *Evictions: Art and Spatial Politics* and the author's overall perspective culminates in the repudiation of an ontology of public space. Instead, for Deutsche, public space has to be redefined each and every time a new subject enters the terrain of debate over the uses of this space; she chastises those who persist in upholding the fantasy of a unified public realm.

W.J.T. Mitchell had already argued in 1990 that 'the pulling down of public art is as important to its function as its putting up'.[12] But given the question posed earlier over what it was in the particular cultural moment that led to the conceptualization and consequent realization of *House*'s 'pulling down', we can now detect in the political unconscious that lies repressed (as so much dead space) in the artwork itself, the premises of the latter's own expendability. For *House* to acquire its full meaning as a late twentieth century landmark public art piece, *it had to be pulled down*. For all its emphasis on space, public art performs best as memory – real or imaginary. Moving beyond the meaning of this particular artwork as yet another manifestation of postmodern difference, we can now begin to reflect on the cultural and social specificity of *House*'s contradictions. *House* became deeply meaningful – secured its position in history – in the same way that historical events nowadays do: retrospectively, after they 'end'. This says as much about the public's relation to public art as it does about the contemporary subject's relation to history. The act of remembering is often used to compensate for the constraints of participation in our social space of 'unrealised democracy'[13] and the inability to act as historical agent. I would argue, however, that these contradictions do not necessarily inhabit the ambiguous terrain of public art for, to quote Mitchell again, 'either there is no such thing as public art, or all art is public art.'[14]

For those familiar with Whiteread's work and her concept of casting space, *House* must have been a natural, anticipated move, transferring the principles of *Ghost*, 1990,[15] the cast of a Victorian room, to a larger scale and succumbing to the allure of site-specificity. To refer to *Ghost* as an origin of sorts already establishes a link between *House* and the uncanny. The association was not of course lost to commentators who saw *House* as a death mask of the real building that had once stood in its place.[16] Performing as a death mask, *House* was an exercise in Adorno's negative dialectics: its success was, first, its failure to represent the object which it had attempted to map as precisely as a cast and, second, the flash of recognition of the abyss separating reality from representation in light of this failure. *House* was a monument to the impossibility of bringing back the dead as well as to the impossibility of adequately representing them. In this sense *House*, as with Whiteread's work in general, can be apprehended in terms of a disturbing repudiation of traditional forms of realism, an obsessive reiteration of realism's impossibility and even undesirability. This may amount to a definition of postmodern aesthetics for some but the truly uncanny difference in Whiteread's art is that such a negation does not leave us in the mercy of the free-floating 'fragment' but in the horror of a complete, hermetically sealed structure. Whiteread's world is not one of parts. (Thinking of parts, even *Ghost*, the lonely room, takes on the principles of a suffocating little universe into which one can peer from the cracks, or rather, seams.)

But of course the strange surfaces of *House* are best understood as surreal rather than real structures. Following closely, and possibly unconsciously, the surrealist 'big idea' of unexpected encounters (here the encounter between the casting materials and those of the real house), the surface of *House* becomes the trace of a process that is simultaneously birth and death, creation and destruction. An association with the grotesque, in our initial misrecognition of *House* for a house, necessarily springs to mind: is it a house or isn't it? And if, as it has been said, the surface is best perceived as a boundary between two worlds (let us call them, for the sake of simplicity and for the purposes of our argument, 'inside' and 'outside'), it can also be perceived as the peculiar space where these worlds collide. This alone suffices to establish the uncanniness of the surfaces of *House* to which we have access. Encounter equals contact. And one of the reasons that the Surrealists so emphasized the significance of the encounter is, as put by Margaret Cohen, that 'against an understanding of representation as visual reflection [*realism*], surrealism proposes that the artist enters into direct *contact* with the reality to be captured.'[17] In the case of *House*, not only the artist but the whole construction team (37) (who finally had to leave the tomb-house through the roof) came into contact. For its visitors *House* itself remained, in the duration of its materialization, both an index of this encounter and a peculiar portal to the warped space of its twisted, inside out, reality. That this amounted to a violation of the real object may not be initially self-evident. But it comes into sharp focus when one thinks of Nabokov's glum hero, Humbert Humbert, whose wish was to turn Lolita's body inside out so as to love its 'interior'.[18] And it's worth pointing out that Anthony Vidler has recovered the tracks of a formidable body of literature where houses are seen as bodies. This may provide a first clue as to this particular sculpture's lack of innocence. Late twentieth century art has long since given up considering the implications of the paradigms of abjection that it has habitually imposed on its audiences. The above considerations do not yet exhaust the horrors of *House*. Vidler detects the true horror in the conclusive fact of the 'domestic' subject's permanent expulsion:

> Thrust so unceremoniously into the void, the domestic subject no longer finds a shell, clinging, as if to Gericault's raft, to the external surface of an uninhabitable and absolute claustrophobic object, forced to circulate around the edges of a once womblike space...where even the illusion of return 'home' is refused, the uncanny itself is banished...the domestic subject is finally out in the cold forever.[19]

36   *House*, 1993

Vidler's perceptive comment captures a great deal of *House*'s true horror. Deutsche's spatial politics of inclusiveness, outlined in her utopian model of a perpetually reconfigured public art, do not seem to apply in this case. Vidler uncovers the deep meaning of *House* as a transcendence of the private/public division that is however replaced by a qualitatively different – much more rigid – distinction between spaces. *House* envelops, and by doing so *produces*, the space to which one can no longer return. For all its concreteness, *House* is a mirage, a phantom. Whatever is around is the space that really exists: the 'real' space that is all we have. Forcing such a sharp distinction between real space and phantom space is perhaps the sculpture's greatest achievement but also a feature that curiously separates it from contemporary exercises in the domestic uncanny.

To take an example from contemporary literature, Mark Danielewski's *House of Leaves*, 2000, offers a quintessentially uncanny story of domestic spatiality. The labyrinthine plot of essentially two novels (one unfolding in the 'supplement' space of footnotes) is also a meditation on the contemporary fascination with the study of space, a term currently characterized by its conceptual or even epistemological indeterminacy. Crucially, the first instances of spatial distortion in the novel begin to register with the protagonists when they discover that the dimensions of the interior of the house do not correspond to those of its exterior. Something is happening in precisely that boundary-surface which also provided Whiteread's focus. The novel will, later on, spiral into a full-blown horror story as domestic space expands and contracts, twists and turns, having acquired a will of its own. It becomes pure space and it is this subtle transition from a previously definable space (domestic) to a mutation of *space for space's sake* that appears so monstrous. Given that the novel also provides an extraordinary critique of the inadequacy of contemporary visual media (in this instance video) as tools with which to record the ever accelerating movement of space, the reader is confronted here with nothing less than the cumulative effect of spatial mutations and interpenetrations which have long been seen as the salient feature of a 'postmodern' world.

To return to the visual arts, Eija-Liisa Ahtila's celebrated film *The House*, 2002, offers a similarly uncanny account of domestic space. Here we watch a young woman narrating and acting out at the same time her experience of distortions of space and time in her house. The house can no longer protect her. Its walls do not keep away the stimuli and data of the outside world. She tries to reinforce the house's resistance to the outside by hanging dark pieces of cloth in front of the windows but this is a futile act. In one of the film's most stunning scenes, the woman flies amidst the tree-tops in the vicinity of the house but finally returns to it, using the house's exterior surface as a kind of ladder that helps her reach the provisional safety, but also spatial boundary, of the ground. Based on accounts of women who have experienced psychotic episodes, the film nevertheless acquires an uncanny relevance for a contemporary audience. It is impossible not to relate its discontinuous narrative with theoretical accounts of postmodern space, especially in terms of an invasion of domestic space by the 'outside' world. But given that it is the house that helps the woman get 'down to earth', in a literal sense, the relationship to domestic space is one both of love and of hate.

In attempting to locate *House* within a wider framework of references, the above examples constitute merely two cases in which contemporary practices of representation (Lefebvre's 'representational space')[20] engage with the intricacies of domestic spatiality. And it is curious enough that in the process a certain demonizing of this spatiality occurs. Even in the relatively sober (because explicitly politicized) feminist critiques of domestic space – from 'Womanhouse', exhibited in the early 1970s in California (where we encounter a woman built into a closet), to Pam Skelton's painting series 'Groundplans' exhibited in the late 1980s in London (where the figure has been partially absorbed, eaten up by space) – domestic space is represented as both disturbed and disturbing. Domestic space is the outcome of a Lefebvrian 'spatial practice' by and through which the identity and lived experience of a certain kind of space is produced and reproduced, not as a meaningless act but as a historically dictated necessity. Similarly, it is hardly accidental that contemporary practices of representation reiterate the horrors of domestic space.

But what do these attacks on domestic space reveal about the nature of our lived reality? The exaggerated unhomeliness of *House*, where the subject is 'finally left out in the cold' opens a different route to this enquiry, principally because of its afore-mentioned difference. Whereas Ahtila and Danielewski draw the subject 'in', into what could be called the domestic in the expanded field,[21] Whiteread's *House* shuts it out. It shuts it out into the public space, which is thus implicitly redefined as the place where one does *not* want to be. Deutsche's positive account of a public space that is, or should be, welcoming to the subject – any subject – is undermined. The unhomeliness of *House* can be seen to reflect, in a pre-eminently distorted way, the alienation one experiences today in the public 'sphere'. The failure of contemporary public spaces to be perpetually reconfigured is the uncanny but elegant solution of the equation that *House* resolves: there is no place where one actually wishes to be. Not in the early 1990s and not today, not in the West and not anywhere else. This is possibly what is witnessed in the tragedy of contemporary asylum seekers in the west – subjects left out in the cold *par excellence* – who, knowingly or unknowingly, aspire merely to get to a place that is *not as bad*.

The 'local' debates that emerged around *House* in London in the early 1990s have nowadays become more globally relevant than ever. The issues are commensurate with efforts to appropriate and re-appropriate public space in the light of aggressive 'development' projects; with the spectre of failed democracy haunting western societies; with the emergence of new subjects through struggles that have challenged both progressive and reactionary certainties; and ultimately with efforts to account for the increasingly complex concept of 'art' as a form of historically determined intervention, as well as the subject/s it addresses or even constructs in its process of becoming (or, in the case of *House*, extinction). The persistence of these major issues and the continuity of the debates between then and now unsettle any facile distinction between the 'postmodern' 1980s and early 1990s, and the present. *House* and its memory are squarely positioned at the heart of these debates. The artwork's relevance to politically engaged understandings of the present and a 'contemporary moment' in the arts has much to do with this fact.

Most importantly, theorizations of postmodern space and culture at large have made audiences less eager to question the still ubiquitous doxology of 'unfixed' meaning. This is especially true of privileged audiences whose access to specific languages and discourses have made them more 'exposed', as it were, to

121

such theories, perhaps elevating them to the level of an unconsciously operating ideology. Being 'unfixed' remains associated with postmodernism. However, discussions of the postmodern are no longer so prominent, and one cannot but wonder about the meaning of this 'disappearance' that remains more mysterious than that of *House*. Is it because the world has actually changed or do we now inhabit the 'core' of a postmodern era and thus lack the critical distance to proceed to even more elaborate dissections of our (post)modern body?

According to a recent self-consciously political account of contemporary art – the exhibition and accompanying platforms of Documenta XI in Kassel – the world has not changed since the early 1990s, when *House* lived and died. In 2002, Documenta XI seemed to demonstrate an aggravation of a global condition of discontent which art is called to document. In this instance documentation clearly amounted to a form of intervention. The most obvious issue identified was, predictably, the encroachment of public space by capitalist ventures under the guise of development. Documenta XI was a monumental testament to local and global opposition to such appropriations of space, suggesting that numerous groups of artists today dedicate their efforts to involving local communities in the struggle against the appropriation of public space by capital. Questions of citizenship and agency were very much on the agenda. Although the artistic director's essay in the exhibition catalogue discussed the emergence of a new subject – Hardt and Negri's idea of 'multitude'[22] in its alliance with the postcolonial subject – as the new locus of resistance on a global scale, one's close attendance to the projects themselves revealed that more traditional forms of identity (as well as 'old battle formations') have hardly abandoned the historical scene. There seemed to be a discrepancy between the invocation of a meta-subject (the multitude) and the documentation of specific forms of social antagonism enacted in the context of artworks that were strongly reminiscent of *House* in its engagement with public space.

I hardly need to remind readers of the ideological and material struggles that were highly visible in the 'sphere' of art in the last quarter of the twentieth century. My interest in those arguments, however, has to do with the complex issues that arose in the context of such struggles, and with the position that *House* occupied –

37   Photograph taken during the making of *House*, Autumn 1993

and still occupies – within those debates. There is extensive documentation of the public's responses to the physical presence of *House* – not to mention the media's well-documented negativity. 'Wot for?' and 'Why not?' were two of the questions marked on the surface of *House* – the point of the encounter. Those questions are still the haunting echo of the debate about 'whose space' is claimed, and 'in whose name' urban space is transformed.[23] The debates, laconically expressed through the juxtaposition of these two questions, brought to the fore the unclear relationship between public art and, simply, 'art'. Whose space did this public art piece occupy? And in whose name was the art of the late twentieth century made? Difficult questions to answer by any means.

The first web of contradictions in which *House* found itself, or was perhaps even consciously positioned within, is defined to an extent by two distinct but interrelated projects of documentation which underpinned its production. On one level, the impenetrable space of *House* was the culmination of its process of coming into being. If conceptual art had often been accused of a repudiation of 'effort' and 'artistic skills' (Carl Andre's *Equivalent VIII*, 1966, and Mary Kelly's *Post-partum Document*, 1976, were two well-known examples of the philistine publicity propagated by media populists), *House* was a telling return to painstaking 'process' that required substantial skill and collaborative effort for its realisation. But the product of that process was wholly ungratifying for those who expected something 'beautiful' to emerge. The outcome of artistic skill and effort was in this case the physically imposing trace of the process itself. Stripped of any (superficially) decorative elements that would not have been produced in the course of its 'birth', but would have had to be added later, *House* came to function as a record of its own becoming.

In doing this however, *House* also exposed the still prevalent myth of the work of art as something that, momentarily at least, disrupts our current condition of alienation. In this sense, *House* occupied – and thus exposed – the often narrow line dividing self-referential medium-focused artistic practices and those *other* artistic practices that consciously distance themselves from the absurdity of 'art for art's sake' to intervene in social spaces. *House* embodied the myth of 'pure' art (myth as 'depoliticized speech', following Barthes) at the same time that it refused to be contained by it. In that sense, *House* was a profoundly political artwork. Crucially, this had less to do with the intention of the artist, who nevertheless saw *House* as a political statement,[24] and more with the fact that it exposed the *currency* and *persistence* of the myth of art for a divided public and a divided press.

Arguably, had this not been the cast of a house but of another object, the responses might have been different. To erect an inaccessible dummy of a previously habitable house in an East London neighbourhood in the early 1990s made a really big deal out of 'homelessness'. For the defenders of the fantasy of 'aesthetic detachment' and of an art solely concerned with its own conditions of being, this was the true horror of *House*: it made manifest in an absolute and irrevocable way the fact that an ultimate transcendence of the social was not possible. Somehow, a powerful 'content', the issue of homelessness, had found its way into the purity and sculptural whiteness of the 'materials', yet at the same time this social abjection was as much outside of *House* as were the rest of us. The materialities that *House* articulated – in its mute way – were of an extremely complex nature. *House* was pure art, but it was also an intervention in social terms. The discursive revealed itself as profoundly material.

Furthermore, *House* played upon the intersection of private and public, a major preoccupation of modern and postmodern art. As a public sculpture, its existence demanded the demolition of an original 'private' space. Of course the house that Whiteread and commissioning agency Artangel Trust had chosen was destined to oblivion anyway – it was to be demolished in order to make room for a park for the benefit of the 'public'. For some, *House* was usurping part of this space for the pleasure of the 'leisure' classes that flocked to see it. Furthermore – a second instance of the sculpture's lack of innocence – *House* had not 'exposed' just any domestic space to the public. It had exposed a working-class domestic space, by enclosing it, turning it inside out, and adding insult to the injury of its scheduled demolition for the greater 'good'. It is unlikely that the project could have taken place in one of London's 'leisure class' neighbourhoods, simply because such neighbourhoods are rarely in need of, and consequently rarely undergo, such radical transformation.

125

David Harvey has argued that 'to materialise a space is to engage with closure (however temporary) which is an authoritarian act.'[25] He might as well have been referring to *House*, a project in which the literal materialization of space, however temporary, was its essential logic. Harvey concludes: 'The history of all realised utopias points to this issue of closure as both fundamental and unavoidable, even if disillusionment through foreclosure is the inevitable consequence. If therefore alternatives are to be realised, the problem of closure (and the authority it presupposes) cannot endlessly be evaded.'[26] Today, living in the aftermath of the 1990s, the problem which faced *House* appears obvious: the early 1990s in east London, as well as in other parts of the world, was experienced as an era without alternatives. Or at least this appears to be a dimension of the political unconscious that *House* threatened to draw back to the surface of consciousness like the corpse of utopia. In an absurd role reversal, *House* was the Medusa of Greek myth (complete with a symbolically blocked womb, according to Vidler) who had herself turned into stone when her stare had been reflected by the apathetic faces of the 'multitude', occasionally animated by the promise of a public 'scandal'.

House then intervened in public space by offering a blow to the utopian aspirations of the latter. The work's implications reached beyond the circuit of 'local histories' to reveal, in all its melancholy, the big picture: a class-divided public space in the context of which some private spaces were far more susceptible to the laws of the capitalist spectacle than others. (Even in terms of scale, a modestly sized working class residence was a more obvious choice for casting than a country house or a Holland Park mansion.) The contradiction here is that *House* stood as a sign of the very condition – a class-divided society – which had enabled its coming into being. In that sense however, its existence was both utopian and dystopian. Utopian because its presence disproved dominant narratives of postmodern aesthetics (very much in vogue in the early 1990s) which equated an emphasis on the local and micro-political with an inability to posit a collective subject of address, or even connect with 'grand narratives'. Dystopian because the means of doing this involved the reinstatement of a predictable form and kind of spectacle, exoticizing a working-class geography by turning it into a sublime encounter with the uncanny.

If that was met with a certain resistance, let us not forget that the Surrealists also found themselves between a rock and a hard place when on the one hand they disrupted the experiment of abstraction and, on the other, rejected the naïvely conceived, populist realism favoured by their more down to earth comrades. *House* continues, and extends, the Surrealist legacy, not out of nostalgia for the experiments of a bygone culture of resistance but because the contradictions defining our contemporary moment and its art – not too far down the road from the contradictions that both produced and destroyed the avant-garde – are necessarily among its materials. However, to paraphrase Jameson, this is hardly surrealism without an unconscious.[27] The allegedly 'dead space' of *House*'s interior activated a surrounding social space animated by the desire of resistance – despite the lack of consensus over what one should resist. Indeed the controversy around *House*, a controversy in which the artwork's specific 'form' and spatiality acquired an additional symbolic dimension, suggested that at least a particular kind of art can still function as a focal point for the rethinking of collective identities.

127

38   *Water Tower* 1998–99, resin cast of interior of water tank, 340cm (134in) x 244cm (96in) diameter

CHAPTER 6

AS THE WEATHER

PAMELA M. LEE

The day I pay a visit to see Rachel Whiteread's *Water Tower*, 1998–99 (38, 39, 41), is, appropriately enough, a rainy day. Not just a mild drizzle, nor even a vigorous shower, but a lashing: it is the kind of rain that moves sideways, the kind of rain that hurts, a relentless pour that calls to mind descriptive short-hands such as 'force of nature'. I am meeting a friend on the corner of Grand and Broadway – Whiteread's work is sited on top of a building at 60 Grand Street – and from there we've planned to set upon a beloved New York ritual: to trawl the area bounded by Houston and Canal Streets to the north and south, and Lafayette and West Broadway to the east and west. We are, in short, seeking passage through the area known as SoHo in an effort to track the comings and goings of that larger, ambient, phenomenon known as the 'Art World'. *Water Tower* will serve as the starting point for our expedition that day, if the rain doesn't put a stop to it.

My friend arrives soon after and we immediately seek shelter. Because neither of us live in New York anymore, having long since taken flight for the West Coast, our knowledge of various places to retreat in SoHo – a good café perhaps? – is not especially up-to-date. By chance we find safe haven in the form of an art bookstore. Waiting for the deluge to pass, and feeling our clothes dry into stiff folds, we settle in for close to an hour. Methodically we make our way through stacks of magazines, new exhibition catalogues on the latest thing, monographs on every up-and-comer and contender. Flipping through the glossy pages, we laugh at our relative ignorance about the current state of the field. '*Who are these people?*' we ask ourselves, two art historians supposedly in-the-know. But we are determined to know. That is the point of our mini grand tour, which Whiteread's work will introduce.

The weather eases up momentarily and we venture out to find the architecture of SoHo in all its sodden, diminished glory: soft-shouldered curbsides are flooded, cobbled streets take on a brackish, oily sheen, the scumbled façades of the old cast-iron lofts are glazed with rain. The few brave souls to have emerged step gingerly across the rushing currents of grey, each forging their slow and resolute paths to whatever destination they're seeking. We have only a few short blocks to get to ours, at which point we do what Whiteread hopes the canny passerby might do: we look up.[1] And there, alternately emerging from and submerged into the storm-tossed expanse of the sky, the work, just barely, comes into view.

Water Tower, indeed, is much less imposing than we thought it would be and much less pronounced than it looks in pictures. It neither proclaims itself against the choked Manhattan skyline nor rails against the weather. Fabricated from translucent resin, it sits on its steel truss, sited on a roof six stories up, and absorbs its environs like a piece of litmus paper. At twilight, as I will discover on another visit, it takes on an incandescence; and that wan light allegorizes a larger phenomenon at work around it, a historical passage or transition. For Whiteread's sculpture will merge with the time of the day and the movement of weather. As the weather this day goes – murky, endlessly drear – so too does the site work. From our worm's-eye perspective down below, it reads like negative space embossed against negative space, all ground and no figure. Unlike those works with which Whiteread established her career in the early nineties, *Water Tower* is a figure of translucency. There is none of the material obstinacy of the earlier work, none of its opacity. A pale slip against the sky, *Water Tower* is a deliquescent, subliminal presence: whatever its actual density and weight (it weighs in at a mere four and a half tons) it looks like it might drift away. Or perhaps, better put, dissolve into the torrential rain.

We take in the sight for as long as we can stand the rain and then move on. And move on we must, for it becomes clear, after making our systematic trek down SoHo's most trafficked and vaunted corridors – Mercer, Greene, Prince, West Broadway – that there is less art to see than we had hoped. Not just because the weather bars our passage, mind you. There are forces at work only slightly less powerful than nature that will keep us from surveying the current crop of new art.

Because, at first slowly, but then with seemingly inexorable force, galleries will give way to retail stores, offering commodities of a different kind. Art will give up the ghost.

We could put it like this: as the weather goes, so goes *Water Tower*. And just as *Water Tower* goes, so too will the world of which it is a part. *Water Tower*, it turns out, will stand as an unwitting figure to the movements and circulation of the art world. It will both index and presage a peculiar change in the weather: the passage not only of the particular world it occupies, but of a kind of work that for a long time had been the centre of it – the site-specific, public work of art.

The story I have just recounted, apart from just being a hapless personal anecdote, details a movement of sorts, not unlike the rain that fell that day nor the water that courses through those ubiquitous pieces of urban architecture known as water towers. My story registers a double passage of not one, but two cities, and the horizon of worldliness *Water Tower* will stage relative to the movements of contemporary art. It is as much a narrative, then, about the art world as it is of the two cities instrumental in shaping that world for the last two decades: New York and London. By extension, it will come to represent a condensed history of site-specific art – art made for a particular place that is alleged to reflect upon the character of that place – and so speak to that work's status in the present. *Water Tower*, of course, is not a sociology lesson. It does not – it could not – offer direct commentary on economic circumstances that would only become legible with hindsight. Nor, as we shall see, was the work site-specific in any doctrinaire sense. But the history of its production, and the longer history to which it both points and belongs, dramatizes the very situation it seemed to forecast before the fact.

The story behind *Water Tower* begins in 1994, when Whiteread was approached by New York's Public Art Fund (PAF) to create a work for the city.[2] For some twenty-five years, the venerable non-profit arts organization had sponsored the production of art in public places as spectacular as the Jumbotron in Times Square and as lowly as the humble manhole covers embedded in the city's streets. At the time of her initial involvement, the PAF had only supported a handful of projects by foreign artists including Christian Boltanski, Alexander Brodsky and

131

39   *Water Tower Project* 1998, acrylic varnish on screenprint, 76.2 x 55.9cm (30 x 22in)

Ilya Kabakov. And now here was Whiteread, fresh from a scandal. Just a year earlier, the artist had been embroiled in the controversy surrounding *House*. A quick detour around that earlier work allows us to confront the wide net of influences informing *Water Tower*. Indeed, the history and reception of *House* and its site, as we shall see, will read as inversely proportional to the fate of *Water Tower*.

In 1994, Whiteread's name was, though with a certain degree of inaccuracy, foremost among an emerging group of British artists identified under the rubric of Young British Art. The rise of Damien Hirst, Sarah Lucas, Gary Hume and Whiteread, among others, marked a turning point in the international art world.[3] Although the YBA phenomenon is too complex to discuss in the space of this essay – or a footnote, for that matter – it is generally associated with the sixteen artists who first showed together at the exhibition 'Freeze' in 1988. Organized by Hirst, then still a student, 'Freeze' was staged in an abandoned Docklands warehouse, itself a sign of the peculiar economic fortunes visited upon London's East End. Not incidentally, Whiteread's especially conspicuous profile was in no small part due to a work sited not that far from the 'Freeze' generation's warehouse, namely *House*, 1993, a concrete casting of a Victorian terraced house located in E3 (the Bow Road area of the East End). Ultimately, the clearing of the house would cede way to a public common – a bit of greenery amidst the urban grey – and Whiteread was granted use of the structure with the understanding that it would not be permanent. This was all well and good until the walls of the house were pared off, exposing an airless grey monolith. What stood in place of the old Victorian terrace was a mute, funereal presence, an inadvertent monument to the long history of misfortunes visited on the area and the family romances variously played out in its domestic scenes.

In its bleakness of form and scarcity of means, *House* conjured minimalist or brutalist associations for those in the know and images of cinderblocks for everyone else. When *House* first appeared at the juncture of Grove Road and Roman Road in the rather desolate Bow neighborhood, many took it as a trenchant blight on an already blighted urbanscape: an insult to the public good in the form of an oppressive mnemonic trace.[4] The popular press and local council launched increasingly violent attacks on the work and the artist responsible for it. For others the work served as a literal platform for social issues attending this class of architecture. 'HOMES FOR ALL BLACK AND WHITE' read some of the first graffiti sprayed on its side.

That last comment in particular will reverberate with the afterlife of the neighbourhood and its gentrification through art. But at the moment of its appearance, the furore over *House* was exacerbated by yet another uproar in the British press: Whiteread was awarded the prestigious Turner Prize that year. The controversy was compounded further by the destruction of *House* three months after its production, following an ever more vituperative round of debates about whether it should stay or go. Should the sculpture remain on-site, its spectral presence a blank-faced monument to an already conflicted reception history, or should it be relocated elsewhere, or should it be flat-out demolished? Parallels were drawn between the plight of Whiteread's work and Richard Serra's *Tilted Arc*, the infamous site-specific sculpture produced for New York's Federal Reserve Plaza in 1981 and then subsequently destroyed in 1989. Mired in bureaucracy and legal rhetoric, the tortured history of that work's reception would dramatize the most pressing ontological questions around site-specific art. Indeed, Serra rejected the removal of the piece on the grounds that 'to remove it is to destroy it': a statement that neatly crystallizes the contextualizing interpretation of site-specific art, which claims that the meaning of the object is indivisible from the place in which it is situated. With Whiteread's sculpture, the notion that *House* could be 'relocated' was also to raise that question. The answer came in the form of resistance: in spite of strong support from the arts community and even some Bow residents, the work, like Serra's, was demolished.

No drama of consensus would be played out with Whiteread's SoHo project. 'I don't want the water tower to be a controversial project', Whiteread offered, 'I want it to seem like a peaceful moment in the sky, to echo the atmosphere of the city.'[5] For the most part, Whiteread got her wish: the work would remain invisible to the casual passerby and it was largely by chance that those uninformed of the project would stumble upon it. But the conditions that gave rise to *House*, as well as the afterlife of the site, describe something of the cyclical nature by which *Water Tower*, and site-specific sculpture more generally, seemingly functions in the public domain only to be implicated in a deepening spiral of private interests. This model will be brought to bear on the ways in which *Water Tower* was understood as a public work of art as it will attest more broadly to the peculiar migrations of the art world in the present.

Following on the scandal of *House*, *Water Tower* would take close to four years to be realized. After the PAF invited Whiteread to produce a work for the city – 'open-ended, without site or budget' as Tom Eccles, director of the PAF described it – the artist visited New York to scout a suitable locale.[6] Whiteread was dissatisfied with the overtly 'public' nature of many of the places she was shown – a point to which we will return – but she settled upon a motif relatively early in the process. She proposed casting a water tower out of resin, a work that would be visible, if inaccessible, from the street. In addition to conceptual questions about the relative public prominence of the work, the project would also prove extremely challenging for its range of its technical considerations. What kind of resin could be used at such a scale? Who had the technological competency to fabricate the thing? Where would one acquire an old water tower to be used as an outsized cast? (The (American Pipe and Tank Lining Company would help Whiteread secure a twenty-five year old wooden tank.) *Where would one ultimately site the work?* Equally trying bureaucratic scenarios would also emerge in the process.

These factors have been amply documented and I will not rehearse them here. What I *will* dwell upon is the choice of Whiteread's motif for the project – a water tower – with respect to the time and place in which it was ultimately sited: SoHo. These may seem wholly obvious points of reference to contend with in reading the sculpture: they may seem the first principles in the interpretation of site-specific art. It is, however, in the *degree* of their intractability – and the larger cultural and art historical backdrop against which those principles are transformed – that one gauges the work's significance in terms of what I have earlier called its 'horizon of worldliness'. It also suggests the ways in which Whiteread's work reveals the *limitations* of the site-specific model in the present.

To be sure, the literature on *Water Tower* has tended to stress one variable (site, for instance) at the expense of the other (the water tower, or vice versa), a testament to the profoundly complex influences informing any of Whiteread's site specific projects. In the excellent PAF source book for *Water Tower*, for instance, Neville Wakefield treats the thematics of water through sharply drawn epigrammatic prose; whereas Luc Sante briskly narrates the place of the water tower in the popular imaginary of New York City. Molly Nesbit calls the work 'an immigrant': it will speak to shifting notions of what constitutes a city today. What would it mean, she asks, to think about the status of the 'city' relative to the site-specific interests the work might perform? All of these readings, richly textured in their respective ways, illuminate specific features of Whiteread's project *decisively*. They stay within their borders. With the luxury of hindsight and several years of accumulated reception, I want to read these and like features of Whiteread's work in their totality – their intertwining – suggestive as they are of the movements *Water Tower* both registers and forecasts: the virtual circulation of an art world.

A tour into the art historical imaginary of these objects will get us halfway there. The water tower is a motif with a great capacity for both historical and art world symbolization. Whiteread's decision to fill the tank of one with clear resin, resulting in a pale, hollow cast when the original was pulled from its surface, could hardly have been an innocent choice. Casting, after all, was her principal mode of art making. Since the late 1980s, she had cast houses, mattresses, closets, the negative spaces around furniture, things variously spent or exhausted or on the way out. Water towers followed logically on this process. Like the Victorian shell that produced *House*, they are nineteenth century creations.

One would not want to call them outmoded, however. Outmodedness suggests irredeemable decrepitude, an accelerated shelf life, things well past their prime. Water towers, by contrast, are emblems of circulation, metonyms for the task of moving thousands of tons of water to New York's citizens twenty four hours a day. Whiteread has often spoken of her castings in terms of mummification – 'the mummification of dead air' as she once described their effects – but here, the force and fluidity contained by the water tower stands in stark contrast to the mordant stillness suggested by her other works. Likening her objects to bodies and their functions, water towers suggest liquid expenditure, tears, say, or the bladder.[7] As if paraphrasing the circulation of water that courses through them (water being the veritable life-blood of the city), water towers would likewise seem to survey the movements and circulation of that life itself, staged above the city as they are.

For such reasons, it's an unavoidable paradox that these lumpen wooden structures are so arcane in appearance. Built on site and faced in timbers, water towers are a strangely rusticated presence in New York, a city whose relentless pace shows little mercy toward the untimely and historical. 'Water towers as we know them today,' Sante writes, 'started going up around the same time as the last bits of rural Manhattan were being leveled and paved.'[8] The inverse relationship Sante identifies in the history of the water tower – that something goes up just as some-thing else goes down – is the crude calculus behind any kind of urban planning, the economy at the foundation of countless modern building programmes. Yet water towers, perched on rooftops throughout Manhattan, stand as ambiguous sen-tinels to this process, a kind of way station between the rural, the industrial and the postindustrial. They are still operational, still tirelessly in use today (New York's res-idents could little survive without them) but their outworn if enduring appearance betrays a history long since over. Poised on the skyline, as if watching the various comings and goings down below, they train their blank surfaces on the horizon as figures of expectation.

Water towers, then, are split personas in this scenario. Augurs of a sort, they are also over-determined signs. Perhaps it seems odd to speak of water towers as ciphers of expectation or circulation: well before Whiteread got to one, their place in the art world record was already secured. We know them well as supporting play-ers in the iconography of New York urbanism: Andre Kertesz, Lionel Feinenger and other photographers would capture their profiles against the more imposing fig-ures of the cityscape, hardening into the image of mid-century Manhattan.

Not until the 1960s and '70s did water towers accrue significance beyond the purely iconographic or representational. It was then that they would come to regis-ter a certain passage from the industrial to the aesthetic, emblematizing the ges-tures of minimalism and conceptual art in congress with the new artistic investi-gation into site. In the late 1960s, for instance, Bernd and Hilla Becher began producing their photographic typologies of water towers. Since 1959, the Dusseldorf-based couple had been taking pictures of industrial archaeology in Europe and North America – blast furnaces, lime kilns, pit heads, grain silos, etc. – informed by the modernist photography of the *Neue Sachlichkeit* and the exploration of seriality in postwar art. Black and white prints, displayed in rows or in a grid format, captured the image of such objects head-on, absent of all human actors. The evacuation of human presence in these works, it has long been argued, reflects the progressively contested status of the industrial landscape. Like the photographs of August Sander before them, intended to survey the variety of social types and classes threatened by the incursions of modernization, the Bechers' steady and systemic documentation of such edifices is thought to capture the transitional passage of industrialization itself.

Telling, then, that the Bechers refer to such typologies as 'anonymous sculpture', as if these former industrial sites were now redeemed as objects of aesthetic contemplation. Indeed, the expression *'anonymous* sculpture' – the sense that these are objects without authors nor wholly distinguishing features – recalls the artistic innovations of the 1960s and '70s, namely minimalist sculpture and conceptual art. Minimalism, after all, was an art that would conflate the concerns of architectural scale to the sculptural object, here now rendered stark and geometric, outsized, repetitious and generic. It would lean heavily upon the visual codes of industrial manufacture as well; think Richard Serra at Kaiser Steel, for instance, or Donald Judd and his heavy metals. Minimalist criticism, too, placed great stress on the specific encounter between the work of art and its beholder, highlighting the range of spatio-temporal factors that influenced one's approach to the work.

By extension, critics would note that the Bechers' seemingly featureless and generic structures – authorless minimalist objects of a type – would reveal complex levels of difference for all the repetition. Whatever anthropomorphic readings were attributed to these pictures, the exercise was also in keeping with the systems-based and semiotic impulses of much conceptual art, which would stress structure, process and organization at the expense of the figural and representational. The Bechers described the water towers in terms of use, rather than image, of functional typologies rather than inert symbolism. The deadpan, unsentimental character of their prose runs parallel to the structural dimensions of their photographs. 'The water tower is part of a complex system by which water is collected and distributed', they wrote:

> Consisting of a water tank and a tower-like substructure, it fulfills two purposes at the same time: storage and the maintenance of pressure... How high a water tower must be depends on how far the water in stores must be delivered. The size of the tank is determined by the amount of water that must be made available at times of peak demand, by daily variations in consumption, and by consideration of emergencies such as fires and pump failures.[9]

The image the artists paint is less nostalgic than it is clinical. It speaks of pressures, flows and containerization, supply and demand, features outside the conventionally aesthetic and representational. Analyzing the water tower as a typological form, the Bechers dramatize its systemic and transitive considerations; calling it 'anonymous sculpture' underscores a new vocabulary for objects that no longer square with the old traditions. Through its implicit references to both minimalism and conceptual art, and through the captions that accompany these anonymous sculptures in their book *Water Tower,* one of the variables the Bechers implicitly introduce is the function of place, of locality.

This observation is by no means accidental to the larger associations water towers would conjure for the art world of the 1960s and '70s. Indeed, the captions accompanying plates 44–58 in the Bechers' *Water Tower* are a tourist's itinerary through the recently designated landmark district of SoHo: Broome Street, Broadway, Spring Street, Houston, Wooster. These captions confirm Luc Sante's remark that the 'neighborhood which water towers are most closely identified with is SoHo', before he adds, 'not incidentally, many of them are protected by landmarks legislation.'[10] That SoHo is almost reactively equated with the 'art world' – or at least *was* equated with that world – is telling in this light. Its history illuminates the way in which we might understand Whiteread's *Water Tower* as narrating the movement from industrial site to 'anonymous sculpture' and then beyond.

Manhattan's SoHo is a relatively recent invention in the real-estate log of New York City. Considering that 'invention' relative to Whiteread's work, we need to emphasize that SoHo's formative history is coextensive with, even indivisible from, some of what we broadly consider to be the conceptual, and by implication, site-specific art of the sixties and seventies. Only in 1971 was the South Houston Industrial Area, a once-thriving industrial site at the turn of the century, declared a landmark district, its cast-iron lofts designated historical architecture.[11] This was a complete about-face from the history of the region that immediately preceded it. From the postwar era to the early 1970s, the industrial neighbourhood, best known for its sweatshops and light-manufacturing operations, was the epitome of urban blight. The streets were desolate and dangerous at night; the architecture was considered unsuitable to the expanding needs of mass production; and lower Manhattan was progressively evacuated by businesses seeking more affordable and spacious quarters elsewhere. David Rockefeller's Downtown Lower Manhattan Association, formed in 1956, was itself formulating a plan to restructure the area, with the headquarters of the Chase Manhattan bank being critical to this scheme. And Robert Moses's appointment as Chairman of the New York City Slum Clearance Committee in 1949 all but guaranteed that the face of Manhattan would be submitted to the wrecking ball, with the South Houston Industrial Area one target area of concentration.[12] In 1961, his plans to construct the Lower Manhattan Expressway threatened the very heart of Greenwich Village.

There was, of course, another side to the story; one that has been celebrated as the origin myth of SoHo. In tandem with the area's demise as a site of industrial production, artists had come to colonize the neighbourhood, illegally inhabiting the old cast iron lofts from the late 1950s. Property was cheap and the scale of the buildings could easily accommodate the most outsized experiments of the postwar avant-garde. From the early 1960s, when the Artists Tenant Association (ATA) was formed, to the time SoHo was granted historic landmark status, artists would prove critical in transforming a once ruinous neighbourhood into the cultural oasis of Manhattan. It was a narrative of gentrification, supported by the efforts of urban planners and real estate speculators. At the beginning of this transformation, of course, the neighbourhood's spaces bore no resemblance to what we think of as the gleaming boutiques and hygienic white cubes of present day SoHo. Floors were unfinished; walls were roughly hewn; streets remained dark; there were very few places one could grab lunch, let alone a cup of coffee. In short, before the South Houston Industrial Area became SoHo, it was a roughshod and ramshackle place, home to a few early 'alternative' galleries.

For many of its principal settlers, the decidedly informal, even fugitive character of the environment opened onto its greatest artistic possibilities, many of which involved the site itself. Some denizens of the early alternative spaces noted that such places weren't 'pristine', that they were knockabout, social spaces, supporting a level of experimentation impossible in the more institutionalized or 'fixed' arenas of the New York art world. As I have written elsewhere, the artist Gordon Matta-Clark, whose sculptural cuttings of buildings have been compared to Whiteread's castings, could bring both his contractor's expertise and architectural knowledge to bear on this new environment. His cuttings saw the area's buildings as a new medium of a type, from which he would extract and then display fragments of a radically discontinuous history. Although a pioneering figure in the genealogy of site-specific art, Matta-Clark's early work in SoHo – explorations of the spaces left in the wake of industrialization – was hardly unique. Indeed, his activities in the neighbourhood ran parallel to many of his friends and colleagues, who likewise worked on-site in the area in the early seventies and who inhabited the neighbourhood's spaces as both affordable *and* performative. Inflected by the phenomenological interests of minimalism, on the one hand, and the land and systems-based site work of conceptual art, on the other, the work was both conceptually and literally contiguous with site. Architecture was up for grabs. Doors, walls, basements, attics and floors became fertile – because liminal – ground for such investigations; and this was as true for rooftops, and even water towers, as anything else. 'I had a big preoccupation with rooftops in the 1970s', the choreographer Trisha Brown wrote, 'about getting up to this other plateau that is always visible, always right with us, but not often acknowledged - a plateau of possibilities, of horizontal communication that was available but that no one was using.'[13]

141

40   Trisha Brown, *Roof Piece* 1974, photographed by Babette Mangolte

41   *Water Tower* 1998–99

Brown – whose preoccupations led to her *Roof Piece*, 1974 (40) – was right to speak about a 'plateau of possibilities'. The formerly gritty, experimental environment she helped create with her peers would culminate in a glittering boomtown, an institution in its own right, ascendant with the paroxysms that variously seized the 1980s stock market. For what happened to SoHo in the two decades preceding Whiteread's work is its own tale about the postwar rise of the art world. Countless galleries formerly located on Madison or the 57th Street corridor in Manhattan now took flight for downtown: Leo Castelli and Illena Sonnabend would move in 1971. New ones would spring up just as quickly. The explosion of the art market in the 1980s seemed to coincide with the heaviest concentration of galleries in the area. If once the South Houston Industrial Area was impoverished, synonymous with the losses of industry, that image was now supplanted by the gentrifying presence of art – so much cultural capital – in the newly re-christened SoHo. The history of SoHo, in other words, makes literal the metaphorical passage described by the Bechers though the form of water towers. The forces of industry had ceded ground for 'anonymous sculpture', from the minimalist and conceptual gestures of the sixties and seventies to the white cubes of the gallery space that followed in their wake.

Against this history, as invisible to the casual visitor to the neighbourhood as Whiteread's work was to the uninitiated, *Water Tower* made its appearance. When the work was hoisted by crane six stories above Grand and West Broadway, SoHo's reputation as the capital of the international art world was well established. By the time of the sculpture's arrival on June 8, 1998, however, something of the ambience of the neighbourhood had changed. An element of its character had gone missing. Ironically, it would take an outsider to provide a commentary on that changed atmosphere.

Maybe it was the first J. Crew to have set up shop that sounded the warning. Perhaps that particular clothing store – or any number of the other popular retail outfits, boutique hotels, make-up shops and design emporiums that had begun to settle in the area – signalled another turn of the neighbourhood's economic fortunes. 'SoHo is becoming common', one commentator remarked. 'Too many outer-borough kids and tour groups thronging the streets and buying shoes and incense, but not $35,000 sculptures.'[14] The heady days of art mercantilism that marked the 1980s, to say little of the fledgling character of the 'alternative' '70s, had passed. Whiteread's work would both augur and capture that movement, just as it captured the movements of weather.

There was no shortage of reviews about Whiteread's sculpture, but the canniest viewers of *Water Tower* seized on its elegaic or melancholic mood. Confirming Whiteread's aspirations for the piece, they also remarked that a sense of calm or even peacefulness suffused the work. That calm, though, might stand for resignation, the peace experienced when acquiescing to one's place in the world. Both Roberta Smith and Robert Storr, two long-time SoHo insiders, argued in separate accounts that Whiteread's work subliminally registered the neighbourhood's passage – 'subliminally' because the work itself did not declare itself in the grand manner of so much site-specific art of the past. In the spirit of earlier readings of Whiteread's work, which frequently turned around the thematics of death, the two treated *Water Tower* as a monument of commemoration: a commemoration of the death of SoHo. 'The sculptural idiom of Water Tower' Storr wrote:

> is perfectly suited to the place and time in which Whiteread has chosen to present it. Art is leaving SoHo for Chelsea and various other urban pockets at an accelerated pace; in its synthesis of a rough-hewn paradigm and elegant state-of-the-art facture, *Water Tower* crowns that increasingly gaudy but depleted district as a kind of *memento mori* of the actions, installations, and spill-over gallery activity that animated SoHo streets in the area's heyday. It is the shimmering echo of the quasi-industrial aesthetic that arose out of that former light-manufacturing zone in the 1960s and 1970s before it became an art mall in the '80s and then, in the '90s, a mall *tout court.*[15]

Smith struck an equally dour note. 'Every swan has its song', she wrote in an article called 'The Ghosts of SoHo':

> New York City's SoHo area is losing out to Chelsea as the center of the downtown gallery scene and filling ever more rapidly with hotels, cosmetics boutiques, home furnishing stores and designer shopping

opportunities. Its farewell melody to the art world may be Rachel Whiteread's self-effacing, site-specific sculpture, *Water Tower*.[16]

Both readings implicitly take the work's site-specific status as a given. Smith is plainspoken about this; Storr more generally subscribes to the notion of site specificity in writing that *Water Tower* 'is perfectly suited to the place and time in which Whiteread has chosen to present it.' That equation, however, presents a paradox. What would it mean to speak of a site-specific work 'perfectly suited to (its) place and time' when the character of that place is deeply unstable? What would it mean to equate a site-specific work with the economic cycles associated with its area – the ascendance, recrudescence and the movements of its markets, whether art, fashion or furniture – when those cycles themselves are perpetually in motion?

A possible response to that question is embedded in Smith and Storr's quotations as well as the acknowledgment of Whiteread's status as a British artist working in downtown Manhattan. Both critics describe how the art world's centre of gravity had shifted by 1998, from the formerly industrial neighbourhood of SoHo to the formerly industrial environs of Chelsea, an area roughly covering 13th Street in the Meatpacking District to 29th Street along 9th and 10th Avenues.[17] That lower West side neighbourhood had of late been the sanctuary to which many galleries sought refuge from SoHo. For some time, dealers had complained about the tourists, the circus-like atmosphere at weekends, the unsavoury, if unavoidable, commingling of art and consumer culture in SoHo. Paula Cooper, among the first to open a gallery in SoHo in 1971, was also among the first to jump ship: she purchased a warehouse in Chelsea in 1995 and hired architect Richard Glucksman to do the renovations. Matthew Marks had also moved his base of operations from Madison Avenue to Chelsea, having arrived in 1993. By 2002, close to 170 galleries occupied the neighbourhood.

This is not to say that the gentrification of Chelsea was anything like the redevelopment of SoHo that preceded it by some thirty years. Indeed, Chelsea's settlement by gallerists was a far hue and cry from the squatter's ethos of SoHo's early history: in 2001, a few years after Whiteread's work appeared across town, ground level space in Chelsea went from $35 to $90 a square foot.[18] What the success of

146

SoHo underscored for the dealers was a new understanding of art and of the matter of property rights as well as the potential liabilities that came with that partnership. As the Director of the New York-based Center for an Urban Future offered on Chelsea: 'Everyone is fearful of the demon of Soho-ization... You have this Darwinian progression: artists move into a neighborhood, prices tend to go up and the artists have to move out.'[19]

However Darwinian the evolution of Chelsea, *Water Tower*'s reception seemed a curious inversion of earlier site-based practices relative to the area's development. In fact Whiteread's work could be seen to reverse the terms of site-specific art, as if *Water Tower* both memorialized and *anticipated* the changing fortunes of the site: we need to remind ourselves that the artist arrived at the motif of the water tower *before* she had actually discovered the site. That the water tower itself suggests a 'figure of circulation or expectation' or a 'way station' of sorts was in keeping with the history of SoHo in its development from an industrialized wasteland to the pivot point of the international art market. By the same token, the work implicitly pointed the way to Chelsea. Whiteread's understanding of these conditions is crystallized in one section of *Looking Up* in which the artist documents her search for a suitable location for the sculpture. Several pictures of sites in Chelsea are included – ranging from the rooftop of the DIA Center for the Arts to an outsize gas station – as are a couple of snapshots of rubbish taken in the neighbouring West Village. As Tom Eccles reports on Chelsea's changing fortunes and the potential relationship of *Water Tower* to it: 'a magnificent (site) in Chelsea, sighted from Dan Graham's installation on the Dia Center rooftop, became a possibility for the project only to slip from our reach due to the expeditious redevelopment of the area.'[20]

With this observation, Whiteread's work seems to prefigure the movement of the New York art world – and the London art world by extension. It did so, paradoxically, through suggesting the new terms (or perhaps limits) placed on the legacies of site-specific sculpture in an increasingly globalized art market. *Water Tower* may have stood as a figure of circulation, yet it would find its ultimate home in the permanent collection of New York's Museum of Modern Art; an acquisition doubtlessly supported by curator Robert Storr, whose writing on *Water Tower* was a

147

thinly veiled paean to SoHo's art world demise. At roughly the same moment as this transition was happening in New York, however, London's East End was also undergoing a sea change that itself seemed foreshadowed by Whiteread's artistic interventions. Whiteread's *House,* after all, drew attention to a neighbourhood subjected to the movements of urban decay and gentrification. A few years after the work came down, the larger scene of the controversy would play site to the concomitant rise of the British art world. As one observer put it:

> In Britain, the intersection of this nostalgia for the industrial and the pressure to find affordable space in an over-heated real estate (not to mention art) market has led to boom times in the East End of London, which has established itself as something of a mecca for edgy art and artists, akin to Chelsea in New York and SoHo before it. With the arrival of Jay Jopling this month and Victoria Miro (unofficially) next month (both of whom are leaving the same West End neighborhood for far larger digs) – not to mention the opening of Tate Modern just across the Thames in May – the movement to the East End is reaching critical mass.[21]

The East End, by this view, came to stand for Britain's version of Chelsea, just as Chelsea had assumed the role formerly held by SoHo. And Whiteread's art would forecast the movement of both scenes. If the construction and destruction of *House* marked the beginning of an era for London's East End, the work that followed signalled the end of an era, and a beginning – elsewhere. From industrial site to anonymous sculpture, *Water Tower* served as an accidental weather vane for the international currents – its atmosphere and drift – of an ever-shifting art world.

CHAPTER 7

THE SHIMMER OF INDUSTRIAL FORM
BLAKE STIMSON

That's what I've done. I've become the wall.

Commanding all the moral authority given to those facing death in his 1980 *La Chambre clair*, Roland Barthes declared – with no apparent compunction – that 'everything' was leading to a specific and fundamental 'impotence'. Under pressure from modernity's colonization of the world by representation, humanity was losing the capacity to experience itself unfolding in time. We are increasingly unable, Barthes lamented, 'to conceive *duration*' either 'affectively or symbolically.'[1] The archness of Barthes's melancholic Bergsonism is generally of interest, of course. (Nobody would question that he tapped a soft spot through which photography seems to be perpetually rethought and experienced afresh.) But it is really the hyperbole of his claim that 'everything' somehow serves to threaten this dismal end – this condition of experiencing oneself in the inert or immobile material form of a photograph or a casting or a statistic or an identity – that may be more useful for us now. This, I will argue, is particularly germane in evaluating the meaning and significance of Rachel Whiteread's mute sculptural form. If we allow Barthes his claim that there is some fundamental part of human experience that is losing its means to find expression in the modern world, then that sculptural muteness itself – where 'emptiness becomes matter', in the words of one of the army of commentators on Rachel Whiteread's work – might well be considered a manifestation or symptom of the impotence he describes.[2] We need think only of her Trafalgar Square monument to an empty pedestal for an easy example.

If we are to cede this diagnosis, however, that impotent condition needs to be regarded with a split valence. On the one hand, Whiteread's method of casting, as an analog of the object, rather than carving or assembling sculptural form can serve well enough as a symptom of some general sort of alienation no different from that bemoaned by Barthes in respect of the photograph's indexing of the world and experience. But if this is so, I will argue that it must also serve as a form of grace or distance or dignity or propriety or beauty. That is, the work must be understood as a self-conscious adoption of an inert or impotent condition, a condition of static, enduring rectitude, of a knowing refusal to create or innovate or imagine and instead to willfully and with pleasure conform to the dictates of the object before it. We cannot feel it as alienation, in other words, without also seeing it as a measure of 'adequate distance', as it was once described, or as that calculus of relations that would give beings the capacity to 'get close without violating each other, and to separate without injury', that is, the capacity of the subject to give the object its due.[3] This second emphasis within the work; one that embraces the authority or right of distance rather than laments it, that willingly or willfully adopts the boundedness of bourgeois propriety, I will take to be a necessary and integral component part of the condition or experience that Whiteread describes when she says – as if it were a moment of self-awakening, a moment of enlightenment – 'That's what I've done. I've become the wall.'[4] My goal here will be to consider both of these critical perspectives – Whiteread's sculptural muteness as a symptom of loss or alienation, on the one hand, and that same muteness as an indication of personal attainment or self-realization or enlightenment, on the other – together as if they were one. Combined they provide a richer and more comprehensive account of the lived social totality – that is, the 'everything' that Barthes was trying to describe – and a useful handle on the commanding affective charge and consequent success of Whiteread's distinctive work.

Even with his luminous intellectual reputation and the substantial authority of his personal life in hand, Barthes's response to the problem of representation he identified was an intrepid one. What he proposed (or, really, demonstrated) was a kind of cure for the travesty that concerned him, a way to re-experience the lost duration of the image, a way to repair the alienation. For our purposes, this more radical part of his account is quite different from what is on offer in Whiteread's work and, anyway, we are free to accept his symptomatology without agreeing to the specifics of his diagnosis or to his remedy. After all, it was this last, the cure, which was most critiqued in his little book; whereas his account of the epistemological entropy wrought by mass production had long been an accepted one, indeed by 1980 having become a kind of de facto reality or truism or, even, a cliché.[5] For example, Barthes's account of human experience flattening out under pressure from representation, of everything becoming 'unconcern, shifting, noise, the inessential (even if I am abusively deafened by it)',[6] as he put it, was in the end no different from that of, say, Daniel Boorstin twenty years earlier railing against images as 'the monotony within us, the monotony of self-repetition',[7] or that of Heinrich Böll just a couple of years after Boorstin condemning the photographically-driven image glut as 'a huge clearance sale all at the cost of the human eye', or that of Jean Baudrillard a couple of years later still, in the throes of 1968, decrying the (advertising) image as a 'uniformula', a 'profound monotony', as a 'devolution in the bliss of the consuming masses'.[8] The world as experienced was becoming overwhelmed and over-determined by an inauthentic, externally-directed wash of facsimiles of what it once was and, more importantly, of what it might otherwise be. For want of a better label we might name this larger moment in the history of mass culture criticism 'postmodernism'.

The problem for all of these observers, like all the generations of mass-culture and photography critics before them, was really a function of industrialization, of the mass production of images, but its impact spread well beyond photography as a technological innovation. Indeed it extended to the way in which representation itself was understood and experienced. What was threatened by the technologically-enabled imaging of 'everything' was representation's own conclusion or termination or finale; the moment when it is undone; the moment of its natural death when it is not merely diluted to insignificance by the industrial slough of imagery, but instead is flatly and willfully negated or abrogated or turned on its head or is simply let go, unfettered, to be happily replaced by another. This concluding moment in the image's life cycle is the prerequisite condition by which the subject rules over its objectification, and that moment is itself threatened with extinction insofar as the image endures in a synthetic, prosthetic material form as evidence of 'what has been'.[9] It is the moment of private, unrecorded imagination always and exclusively in flux, of representation unfixed and unbound, of the privacy or death of objectification. It is, Barthes wrote, the 'absolutely precious, inalienable' moment 'where my image is free' – free, that is, 'to abolish itself.'[10] It is this moment that is travestied by the industrialization of image making.

Instead of such a freedom or autonomy, the experience of representation wrought by the power of industry is an experience of the image in chains. Barthes and the others argued that the image was not abolished or exorcized or liberated, but instead repressed and, with its becoming 'noise', becoming ubiquitous, our experience was of the image bound without release to its ever more feeble and tawdry yet ever more interminable life. The industrialized image's problem, in other words, was its obdurate materiality, its reproducibility not only from one iteration to the next across space but over time. Perhaps the best metaphor, one that extends, spoken or not, throughout the postmodernist imagination about image worlds, is the image as *undead*, the image that is unable to rest in peace. This, we might note, is what a ghost is, whether Whiteread's sculpture by that name or any other: it is a form of life after death that persists beyond its natural lifespan. Insofar as that persistence serves melancholy by not letting go, by holding on to the image in lieu of saying goodbye to its original, it assumes the form of a nagging contradiction that forces it, with ever greater exhaustion and a corresponding persistence, to cling to the present. The contradiction that the image suffers as a consequence of its industrial production arises from the space between, on the one hand, the various human intentions involved in the image's making and, on the other hand, that part of the image's intentionality that is born of the machine, the part that arises unguided from the production process itself. Such, Barthes and his fellow postmodernists came to be convinced, was the plight of the image generally in modernity, its damnation by the conditions of its production. Its ghostliness was a function of industrialization, they now realized, not, as Barthes in particular had assumed previously, of mythologization.

As a rule, industrial methods of image making are indeed different from artisanal methods in that they cede control and, with it, content, to the process or method itself. Whiteread's casting process, for example, like photography as Barthes described it, is a form of testimony really, not interpretation or argumentation or polemic or conviction or insight. Like any testimony it can lie by withholding or misrepresenting the truth, of course, but since it is indexical rather than demonstrative in its main claim as a form of representation – since it is grid-like rather than narrative, static rather than dynamic, objective rather than subjective, atomistic rather than collectivistic, passive rather than active – in the process it foregoes some of that autonomy conventionally granted to representation. It produces meaning, for sure, and that meaning, again, may just as well be false as true, but it is meaning born of, and inextricable from, its industrial process; and it carries with it a kind of objectivity – that of the unalloyed declaration, as Barthes put it, of 'that-has-been'. This does not mean that it is without subjective intention. Rather, it is only that the subjective intentionality of the photograph loses ground to the objective material consequence of the industrial apparatus used to pursue that intention. In this way industrial methods of representation such as photography and Whiteread's casting technique have their greatest impact as truth claims: beyond realizing their intended meaning they cannot help but enact a type of semiotic implosion. They cannot help but abstract meaning and, disembodying it, locate it beyond the subjective experience of artist, patron or the model or other human subject represented, and instead place it in the objective productive capacities of the methods of representation themselves.

153

This externalization of subjective experience has always been a function of industrial form. Before the rise of the postmodernist critique of Barthes and the others, it was seen less as a threat and more as an artistic opportunity. Modernism's penchant for the grid as form, for example, or for industrial or commercial materials and methods (such as photography and casting) or, even, for the proletariat or the bourgeoisie as class-subjects or themes, were means for extending art and the experience it offered fully into modernity. In so doing there was a formal embrace of a kind of anonymity in abstraction as the means by which that modernity of representation would be achieved. Meaning, truth and experience were no longer to be realized through empathy or identification by anthropomorphizing the terms of social life – in social imagining made available through the representation of the lives and times of gods or kings, for example, or the bourgeois individual or peasant or proletarian as persona or type, or even through allegories like Liberty or Leviathan – but instead were imagined as abstractions *qua* abstractions. They became a grid or a square or a cube, for example, or an anonymous, personality-free worker-as-cog, or existed in a purified opticality, or purified picture plane, or in the marketplace-random montage of images, or in the theoretically endless reproducibility of mass-manufactured form.

Modernist meaning realized its content as art – even its affective content – as if it were statistical rather than dramatic or literary or musical, as if it were there in the abstraction itself rather than in the welling up of empathy or status, of pride or sorrow or longing or anticipation or any of a variety of other sundry forms of individualized, embodied understanding. It was not the will and action of an individual that held sway as artistic content – the whims or authority or revealed truth of a god or king or bourgeois, for example. Instead art became dominated by the products of a system of relations that could only be observed and understood at a distance, by analysis and calculation, by thinking through large, inscrutable categories abstracted to a condition of theory not available to the untrained eye or mind: 'industry' or 'painting', 'class' or '*l'art pour l'art*', 'market value' or 'aesthetic value'. Meaning was understood to be constructed like a machine and was not a function of individual consciousness or affect or intuition or reason or will or desire but instead could only emerge through abstract systematicity. Truth and beauty alike could only be conceived in their modernism by being particularized as 'isms' and meaning as such was threatened with a kind of alienation or dehumanization or desacralization or disenchantment. There was a kind of entropic devolution from the old experience of collective communal subjectivity into the new particulate of systemic, objectified self-understanding: into, that is, the relations of production. Meaning, in other words, was abandoning its status as revelation by becoming rationalization, abandoning its status as self-realization, as the coming into faith or enlightenment or embodied *durée*, and becoming the brute, calculable, cog-like purity of a photograph or a casting or a statistic or an identity. Meaning for modernism was (or at least threatened to be), as Hegel had diagnosed it already in 1807, 'the return of consciousness into the depths of the night in which 'I' = 'I'.'[11]

The epistemological contest of modernity has always been a battle over which figure, the subject or the object, should govern the other and it is into this fray that all modernisms dive, particularly so those that come closest to the economic base by deploying the mechanical processes of industrial method. The question for any art practice *qua* modernism is really about how it handles the rationalization of inner-worldly life, the transition from a religious or pseudo-religious worldview to a scientific or pseudo-scientific one, that is, how they resist or enable it on the level of self-understanding. This has always been the main job of art as modernism. In the end it mediates that transition, it softens or redirects or deflects that blow to the meaning and experience of subjectivity. Insofar as it does this with industrial forms of representation – making art over into a mechanical index of experience rather than an icon or symbol arising organically as 'self expression' or some other form of revelation – it effects that transition in one way or another. 'Whatever else its power', Rosalind Krauss long ago noted specifically about photography but which can just as well be said about Whiteread's casting method (as Krauss herself has more recently intimated), it defines itself by 'ceding the language of art back to the imposition of things.'[12] Of course, this gesture is more often ideological than not and, typically, in all the wrong senses. But when it is done right modernism's language of 'the imposition of things', its ceding of the autonomy of the subject to the object, its externalization of inwardness, its limiting of itself to testimony or to documentation, its minimalism or muteness, has been able to take advantage of the power of abstraction to make history appear no longer as an idealism (as Hegel's *Geist* marching forward on its own volition, for example) but as a comprehensive and dynamic material reality: that is as a system of relations or a kind of machine. It is a tragic enterprise, for sure – it can only achieve this at its own expense, by foregoing Barthes's cure or any other, by holding firm to alienation, to its own self-abnegation – but it is a valiant intercession in our industrialized experience of the world nonetheless. For it is here that we, as bearers of the grand bourgeois experiment, most experience beauty and understanding.

We might reframe the central question of modernism and representation here in its most general form, by simply asking about the function of modern art, about its place in the world. Something of an answer to this question has been associated with Whiteread's work from the beginning. Even she herself, for example, has said that her career-making *House* 'made people aware of what power a piece of modern art can have',[13] and indeed, given its tremendous reception we might well agree that it was powerful, that it did generate great interest, that it did seem to call up some sense of meaning and purpose for modern art. We would not be well served to leave it at that, however. Such a conclusion gives us only a measure of the effect, not an account of the substantive cause or meaning or purpose of that effect. And, of course, such effects can be manufactured by various means and to diverse ends (as we know well enough from the successes and failures of some of Whiteread's YBA colleagues). What then is the source of this power? What sort of claim does Whiteread's work generally make for modern art?

There are a number of interpretations that have been made in the literature, including a variety by Whiteread herself, which might be grouped generally under two headings. First is the idea that she 'casts the places we don't think about', as one observer puts it, that she – like the camera that records the background ephemera that the photographer is not looking at – makes visible that which was always there right in front of us but was somehow hidden from view.[14] Like photography, Whiteread's process records elements of the physical world that were there but which we were not focused on. This phenomenological interpretation has a psychoanalytical extension as well, with Whiteread's work said to break down the hold of repression and make the unconscious conscious. 'She revealed the object's past, its "unconscious", so to speak,'[15] writes one observer, with a second making the claim even stronger by rendering it pathological, that is, as a kind of repression of repression. 'In Whiteread's world, where even the illusion of a return "home" is refused, the uncanny itself is banished.'[16] The second dominant group of interpretations understands the power of Whiteread's work to be not so much embodied as political. This cuts two ways: on the one hand, the documentary function of her work is said to be political because it carries a social residue in the textures and forms lifted from the spaces she casts. On the other hand, the direct documentary function of her casting method is assumed to carry a kind of ideological minimalism, that is, it is assumed to carry the mechanical neutrality often associated with photography even when a strong hand is seen in the composition. 'Rachel stood apart' from her YBA colleagues, notes one newspaper journalist, 'because she was much more a classical, formal stylist than a conceptual artist, with no political or ideological axe to grind.'[17]

The two categories of interpretation – the phenomenological (or psychoanalytical) and the political – are opposite in many respects but they do share an important piece of common ground: both emphasize a distancing from self, a standing apart, a becoming objective rather than subjective, an 'adequate distance', for artistic expression. This, of course, is consistent with our larger theme about the externalization of the inner-worldly enabled by industrial form. The question is whether the inner-worldly is, in fact, simply 'banished' or repressed by the process, as has been suggested, or whether it is retained as a symptom or other condition of its new form, that is, for example, as a measure of psychoanalysis' uncanny or as a measure of the Enlightenment's autonomy, a measure of not ceding control back to the imposition of things. One way to consider the status of the relation between the two realms is to examine the mediation function: that is, to consider the agent that enables the externalization of the internal or the objectification of the subjective realized by the industrialization of expression.

The idea of a mediator between realms of experience that enables the relations of those realms has been around for a long time. The figure of Christ is the prototype – 'For *there is* one God, and one mediator between God and men, the man Christ Jesus' – serving not only as intercessor between worldly and heavenly realms but also as the vehicle through which adherents experience themselves as supra-individual, as part and parcel of a collective subject, as the body of Christ. A central element of this function is that it itself vanishes – that is, mediation happens in the death of the old form (Christ on earth) and the resurrection in a new (Christ seated at the right hand of the Father). In the process a new social relation is set in place. Like Christ, the same has been said of the Public Sphere, of Protestantism, and of Europe – that is, that they enter as historical actors, mediate opposing terms thereby enabling a conversion and then vanish, living on only as a pale memory of what they once were.[18]

These later mediators are different from their prototype by virtue of their modernity, of course: they mediate between social institutions and conventions only, not between heaven and earth, and they conflate the positions of saviour and saved. Indeed, we might say that this vanishing of the mediator is itself a constitutive condition of modernity in a way that it was not for pre-modern Christianity: where Christ's death enabled the adoption of a new identity for Christians, a new sense of self and a new *sensus communis*, the great bourgeois institutions of the Public Sphere, Protestantism and Europe – that is, of the bourgeoisie itself as an identity and a set of values and aims – had only themselves to put on the line (or, as it were, on the cross). The mediation between old world and new, between the experience of meaning as revelation and that of rationalization, between late feudalism and the late capitalism in which we live today, could only be realized by the bourgeoisie through its own self-vanishing, its own self-annihilation. For our purpose, we can illustrate that self-annihilation with one exemplary bourgeois value, the archaic ring of whose name alone should indicate the process we are describing: *propriety*. This value, of course, is inseparable from the value of *property* – both values insist on strict boundaries that distinguish inside from outside – but where the latter institutionalizes an individualized relation to the world, the former does so for a collective one and endows its bearer with the experience of participation in a community of adherents. It is this adherence, this experience of self and of *sensus communis* of the bourgeoisie that has vanished.

Such was the 'impotence' that Barthes described which 'everything' was leading to. The loss, however, was not experienced so much in temporal terms, as Barthes's Bergsonian duration, as it was in spatial terms, as the loss of 'adequate distance'. That is, what was given up as the bourgeoisie abandoned its markers of self, its propriety, was the boundedness that made identity legible, that prevented it from folding into the market as just one more commodity form. This identity has no value unto itself, of course, but what it does provide is the buffer that would allow beings to 'get close without violating each other, and to separate without injury'. That is, it provided the means for the development of political subjectivity, for a system of rules about relating that achieved more than the delimitation of harmful behaviour but instead cultivated new forms of productive human interaction – art itself not being the least of them. Identity for the bourgeoisie was its political moment, its moment on the barricades rather than its moment in the bank. It was its triumphant declaration of itself as reason – *cogito ergo sum*; its triumphant declaration of itself as freedom – *liberté, egalité, fraternité!*; and it was here that its heroic power of subjectivity, rather than the instrumental exercise of reason, gave it its power of objectivity.

The stiffness of propriety that carried on into the twentieth century was the vanishing remainder of the bourgeoisie in this earlier, triumphant subjective moment, the remainder of the passing pre-late-capitalist phase when it had a proper subjectivity, and it is to this residue that Whiteread returns us. It is this, first of all, that allowed her to stand at a distance in the various ways outlined above – the phenomenological and the political – and it is this that allowed her to stand apart from her generation. 'She is more middle class than most of the YBAs and much better behaved', is how one reviewer put it. 'I'm sure she'll be the first of her generation to be made a Dame – actually, I don't see why she hasn't been made one already.'[19] The muteness of Whiteread's sculptural form, its withholding or stopping short of creative daring or the transgression of good taste in its simple indexical technique, is the part that is 'more middle class than most' (whether or not that claim is true, or simply part of a larger mythologizing of the YBAs as working class brats, as successors to punk). It is the part that is more reserved and respectable and appealing. It is the part that is 'socially or aesthetically conventional', as the OED defines bourgeois, or 'conventionally respectable and [*willfully*] unimaginative', or even 'philistine'. In this condition the work's beholder is returned to the perspective of the long-vanished mediator, that is to bourgeois subjectivity with its reserve and propriety, its sense of boundedness and order, its belief in the categories of reason and reasonableness, of respectful conformity to the demands of the space in which it finds itself, its respect for the object it addresses, as a mode of

159

being in the world. In the words of one conservative critic raging against Whiteread being awarded the Turner Prize, her work appeals to those who 'have ceased to appreciate the craft of creation', those 'who have forgotten what they are rebelling against', that is, to those who have forgotten that it was their job to rebel at all.[20]

Such is the effect of Whiteread's work, the answer it proposes to the question about the role of modern art: it commands respect, but respect without affect or intention. This is the respect of reason become identity, of objectivity become subjectivity, the respect of the *cogito*, and it is the province of the machine as much as it is the bourgeois. In so being it folds readily into the noise, monotony, uniformula, etc. that Barthes and the others complained of, into the abstraction or disembodiment or disengagement of meaning. But it also stands on its own as a measure of truth opposite to the simple material reality of the object. This then is the meaning or the charge of Whiteread's method, just as it has routinely promised to be of photography and other industrial forms of representation: the negative or mould taken from life stands on the cusp of interpretation, it flirts with meaning and meaningfulness as its opposite, but never enters into the fray. Fiona Bradley got this effect just about right in her discussion of Whiteread's work, particularly so in her doubling of the term 'other': 'Photography, like casting, combines that which is present with that which is other – the residue of the original which advances and retreats in the mind of the other.'[21]

Meaningfulness shimmers in the mind of the beholder as Whiteread moves back and forth between the then of the original and the now of beholding, between self and other, between the experience of subjecthood and that of objecthood. Becoming the wall, and then immediately the 'I' in that same process of becoming, she quivers with all the potential of understanding, all the potential of self-identification, without ever getting there. This, finally, is the role of the mediator and it is no different in kind from that once occupied by the bourgeoisie with its great institutions of the Public Sphere, Protestantism and Europe: it is the possibility of knowing valorized for itself, as itself. It is, as Hegel had it, to be standing in full view of the 'depths of the night' in which meaning collapses into 'I' = 'I' and holding back, with reserve and propriety and the charm of discretion. This is what the mediator was when it had not yet vanished: 'the one-sidedness which takes as *essential Being* the simple element of thought in contrast to actuality,' that is, the 'one-sided extreme of the Self' that experiences its own abstraction of self as its truth.[22] Whiteread's accomplishment is thus fully individualistic or fully bourgeois but it is so philosophically rather than politically or phenomenologically. The Self that she gives us is neither strictly subjectivized nor objectivized but instead there before our eyes in all its modernism as a moment in systemic understanding, as a necessary corollary to the tawdry industrial remainder of the wall. In this way the alienation that Barthes described is redeemed differently: that is, not as a problem to be solved or a disease to be cured but instead as a condition to be exercised, a circumstance to be enjoyed for the fullness, beauty and enlightenment of its contradiction.

161

CHAPTER 8

RACHEL WHITEREAD'S JUDENPLATZ MEMORIAL IN VIENNA
Memory and Absence

JAMES E. YOUNG

Among the hundreds of submissions in the 1995 competition for a German national 'memorial to the murdered Jews of Europe', one seemed an especially uncanny embodiment of the impossible questions at the heart of Germany's memorial process. Horst Hoheisel, already well-known for his negative-form monument in Kassel, proposed a simple, if provocative, anti-solution to the memorial competition: blow up the *Brandenburger Tor*, grind its stone into dust, sprinkle the remains over its former site, and then cover the entire memorial area with granite plates. How better to remember a destroyed people than by a destroyed monument?

Rather than commemorating the destruction of a people with the construction of yet another edifice, Hoheisel would mark one destruction with another. Rather than filling in the void left by a murdered people with a positive form, the artist would carve out an empty space in Berlin by which to recall a now absent people. Rather than concretizing and thereby displacing the memory of Europe's murdered Jews, the artist would open a place in the landscape to be filled with the memory of those who come to remember Europe's murdered Jews. A landmark celebrating Prussian might and crowned by a chariot-borne Quadriga, the Roman goddess of peace, would be demolished to make room for the memory of Jewish victims of German might and aggression. In fact, perhaps no single emblem better represents the conflicted, self-abnegating motives for memory in Germany today than the vanishing monument.[1]

Of course, such a memorial undoing would never have been sanctioned by the German government, and this, too, was part of the artist's point. Hoheisel's

162

42 *Holocaust Memorial* 1995/2000, Judenplatz, Vienna. 390 x 752 x 1058cm
(154 x 296 x 416in)

proposed destruction of the *Brandenburger Tor* participated in the competition for a national Holocaust memorial, even as its radicalism precluded the possibility of its execution. At least part of its polemic, therefore, was directed against actually building any winning design, against ever finishing the monument at all. Here he seemed to suggest that the surest engagement with Holocaust memory in Germany might actually lie in its perpetual irresolution, that only an unfinished memorial process can guarantee the life of memory. For it may be the *finished* monument that completes memory itself, puts a cap on memory-work, and draws a bottom line underneath an era that must always haunt Germany. Better a thousand years of Holocaust memorial competitions in Germany than any single 'final solution' to Germany's memorial problem.[2]

On a walk he was taking in Berlin's former Jewish Quarter, Christian Boltanski was drawn curiously to the occasional gaps and vacant lots between buildings. On inquiring, he found that the building at Große Hamburgerstraße numbers 15 and 16 had been destroyed by Allied bombings in 1945 and never rebuilt. In a project he mounted for the exhibition *Die Endlichkeit der Freiheit* in October 1990 called 'Missing House', the artist thus set to work retracing all the lives of people who had lived in this 'Missing House' between 1930 and 1945 – both the Jewish Germans who had been deported and the non-Jewish Germans who had been given their homes.[3]

Boltanski found family photographs and letters, children's drawings, rationing tickets and other fragments of these lives, xeroxed them and put them all together with maps of the neighbourhood in archival boxes. At this point, he had nameplates hung on the white-plastered wall of the building next door to identify the now missing inhabitants, Jews and non-Jews – leaving the lot empty. His 'Missing House' project thus became emblematic for Boltanski of the missing Jews who had once inhabited it; as its void invited him to fill it with memory, he hoped it would incite others to memory as well.

In two other installations, artists Micha Ullman and Rachel Whiteread have also turned both to bookish themes and negative spaces in order to represent the void left behind by the 'people of the book'. In order to commemorate the infa-

43   Maquette for *Holocaust Memorial* 1995, mixed media

mous Nazi book-burning of 10 May 1933, the City of Berlin invited Micha Ullman, an Israeli-born conceptual and installation artist, to design a monument for Berlin's *Bebelplatz*. Today, the cobbled expanse of the *Bebelplatz* is still empty of all forms except for the figures of people who stand there and peer down through a ground-level window into the ghostly-white, underground room of empty shelves Ullman has installed. A steel tablet set into the stones simply recalls that this was the site of some of the most notorious book-burnings and quotes the poet Heinrich Heine's famously prescient words, 'Where books are burned, so one day will people be burned as well.' But the shelves are still empty, unreplenished, and it is the absence of both people and books that is marked here in yet one more empty memorial pocket.

In all three of these cases, the artists have broached a question that has, in fact, been central to the preoccupations of other artists like Bruce Nauman and Rachel Whiteread, as well as to philosophers like Levinas and writers like Jabes: how does one give absence a presence and form without violating the memory of loss? More specifically, to what extent will memorials commemorating Europe's murdered Jews always seem to fill in and even compensate the terrible void their murder has left behind? Can such a void be articulated formally without seeming to fill it in with the formal object itself, its meanings and its memory of an absence?

In a 1996 competition for a memorial to the 65,000 Austrian Jews murdered by the Nazis, initiated by Nazi-hunter Simon Wiesenthal, a distinguished jury of experts appointed by the city chose a brilliant, if abstract and controversial, design by the Turner Prize-winning British artist, Rachel Whiteread. In her winning proposal for Vienna's official Holocaust memorial to be located at the Judenplatz, Whiteread proposed casting the spaces between and around books as the memorial figure by which Austria's missing Jews would be recalled (42, 43, 44). The positive cast of the space around books in an anonymous library, the interior turned inside-out, would thus extend her sculptural predilection for solidifying the spaces over, under and around everyday objects, even as it makes the book itself her central memorial motif. But even here, it is not the book per se that constitutes her now displaced object of memory, but the literal space between the book and us. For as others have already noted, Whiteread's work since 1988 has made visually palpable the notion that materiality can also be an index of absence: whether it is the ghostly apparition of the filled-in space of a now demolished terraced house in London (*House* launched Whiteread to international prominence), or the proposed cast of the empty space between the book-leaves and the wall in a full-size library, Whiteread makes the absence of an original object her work's defining preoccupation.[4] Like other artists of her generation, Rachel Whiteread is preoccupied less with the Holocaust's images of destruction and more with the terrible void this destruction has left behind.

Given the thematic preoccupation with absence and voids in all her work, it is not surprising that Whiteread was one of nine artists and architects initially invited to submit proposals for a Holocaust memorial in Vienna. Other invitees included the Russian installation artist Ilya Kabakov, Israeli architect Zvi Hecker, and the American architect Peter Eisenman. But Whiteread was clear from the outset that this work would be both an extension of her previous work and something that would have to stand on its own in a public space, far from any references to her collected oeuvre. 'When I was asked to submit a plan for the Holocaust Memorial in the Judenplatz in Vienna, it was clear to me from the outset that my proposal had to be simple, monumental, poetic and non-literal. I am a sculptor: Not a person of words but of images and forms', she added, before continuing:

167

> One of the aspects that intrigued me about the commission is that it adds a dimension to my work that I have not experienced before. The sculpture will have to function within the framework of my own art, and it will have to comply with what I have done before. At the same time, being a memorial, it takes on a whole new meaning outside my own framework of references. It functions both as private and public space. It has to be seen as a work of art in its own right and yet takes on very specific outside meanings.
>
> The difference between *House* (my only previous monumental public sculpture) and the Judenplatz monument is that *House* was in effect a private sculpture being made public 'by default' (as a result of

its scale and visibility). The Judenplatz monument is from inception
bound up in history and politics.'

After spending eighteen months in Berlin in 1993 and 1994, Whiteread did
not come unprepared to the subject of the Holocaust. I know she saw the exhibition I curated on memorials for the Jewish Museum, which travelled to the German
Historical Museum in 1994, and she has said that her time in Berlin left her preoccupied with both the raw mementoes of the past and the infinite traces of
absence she found everywhere. Little did Whiteread know just how bound up her
piece would become in the city's history and politics, as we'll come to see.

As proposed, Whiteread's cast of a library turned inside-out measures 10
metres by 7 metres, is almost 4 metres high, and resembles a solid white cube. Its
outer surface consists entirely of the roughly textured negative space next to the
edges of book leaves. On the front wall facing onto the square is a double-wing door,
also cast inside out and inaccessible. In its formalization of absence on the one hand
and of books on the other, it found an enthusiastic reception amongst a jury looking for a design that 'would combine dignity with reserve and spark an esthetic dialogue with the past in a place that is replete with history.'[5] Despite the jury's unani-
mous decision to award Whiteread's design first place and to begin its realization
immediately, however, the aesthetic dialogue it very successfully sparked in this
place so 'replete with history' eventually paralyzed the entire memorial process.

For like many such sites in Vienna, the *Judenplatz* was layered with the invisible memory of numerous anti-Semitic persecutions: a synagogue was burned here
in a 1421 pogrom, and hundreds of Jews died in the *autos-da-fe* that followed.
Though Whiteread's design had left room at the site for a window into the archaeological excavation of this buried past, the shopkeepers on the *Judenplatz* preferred
that these digs into an ancient past also be left to stand for the more recent murder
of Austrian Jews as well. And although their anti-Whiteread petition of 2,000
names referred only to the lost parking and potential for lost revenue they feared
this 'giant colossus' would cause, they may also have feared the loss of their own
Christian memory of this past. To date, the sole memorial to this medieval mas-
sacre was to be found in a Catholic mural and inscription on a baroque facade over-

looking the site of the lost synagogue. Alongside an image of Christ being baptized in the River Jordan, an inscription reads (in Latin): 'The flame of hate arose in 1421, raged through the entire city, and punished the terrible crimes of the Hebrew dogs.' In the end, the reintroduction into this square of a specifically Jewish narrative may have been just as undesirable for the local Viennese as the loss of parking places.

In fact, unlike Germany's near obsession with its Nazi-past, Austria's relationship to its wartime history has remained decorously submerged, politely out of sight. Austria was a country that had (with the tacit encouragement of its American and Soviet occupiers) practically founded itself on the self-serving myth that it was Hitler's first victim. That some 50% of the Nazi S.S. was composed of Austrians, or that Hitler himself was Austrian-born was never denied. But these historical facts also never found a place in Austria's carefully constructed post-war persona. In a city that seemed to have little reason for remembering the murder of its Jews, the entire memorial project was soon engulfed by aesthetic and political *Sturm und Drang*. The vociferous arguments against the winning design brought the commissioning process to a grinding halt. Maligned and demoralized, Whiteread resigned herself, she told me, to the likelihood that her memorial would never be built.

But then suddenly, in early 1998, the city of Vienna announced that a compromise had been found that would allow Whiteread's memorial to be built after all. By moving the great cube one metre within the plaza itself, the city found that there would be room for both the excavations of the 1421 pogrom and the new memorial to Vienna's more recently murdered Jews. Nonetheless, the debate in Austria has remained curiously displaced and sublimated. Lost in the discussion were the words one of the jurors and a curator at New York's Museum of Modern Art, Robert Storr, had used to describe what made Whiteread's work so appropriate in the first place. 'Rather than a tomb or cenotaph', Storr wrote:

> Whiteread's work is the solid shape of an intangible absence – of a gap in a nation's identity, and a hollow at a city's heart. Using an aesthetic language that speaks simultaneously to tradition and to the future, Whiteread in this way respectfully symbolizes a world whose irrevocable disappearance can never be wholly grasped by those who

testimony [handwritten marginal note]

did not experience it, but whose most lasting monuments are the books written by Austrian Jews before, during and in the aftermath of the catastrophe brought down on them.[6]

Rather than monumentalizing only the moment of destruction itself, Whiteread's design would recall that which made the 'people of the book' a people: their shared relationship to the past through the book. For it was this shared relationship to a remembered past *[memory-archive]* through the book that bound Jews together, and it was the book that provided the site for this relationship.

Though Whiteread is not Jewish, she has – in good Jewish fashion – cast not a human form but a sign of humanity, gesturing silently to the acts of reading, writing and memory that had once constituted this people as a people. Now that Whiteread's Judenplatz Memorial to Austria's murdered Jews has actually been realized, I think both the city and its Jewish community must be congratulated: the Jewish community for the courage and audacity of its aesthetic convictions, and the city for finally bringing boldly to the surface its previously subterranean shame.

How does a city 'house' the memory of a people no longer at 'home' there? How does a city like Vienna invite a people like the Jews back into its official past after having driven them so murderously from it? From the beginning, planners for the Judenplatz memorial recognized that this would be no mere reintroduction of Jewish memory into Austria's civic landscape but an excavation of a long-suppressed memory. Freud, of course, may have described such a phenomenon best in his reflections on 'the uncanny': 'This uncanny is in reality nothing new or alien, but something which is familiar and old-established in the mind and which has become alienated from it only through the process of repression. (...) The uncanny [*is*] something which ought to have remained hidden but has come to light.'[7] Thus would Whiteread's phantasm generate its own sense of a disquieting return, the sudden revelation of a previously buried past. Indeed, if the very idea of the uncanny arises, as Freud suggests, from the transformation of something that once seemed familiar and homely (such as the Judenplatz) into something strange and 'unhomely', then how better to describe the larger plight of Jewish memory in Austria today?

44   *Holocaust Memorial* 1995/2000, Judenplatz, Vienna

By extension, the memorial uncanny might also be regarded as that which is necessarily anti-redemptive. Indeed, for the artists of Whiteread's generation, the notion either that such suffering might be redeemed by its aesthetic reflection or that the terrible void left behind by the murder of Europe's Jews might be compensated by a nation's memorial forms is simply intolerable on both ethical and historical grounds. At the ethical level, this generation believes that squeezing beauty or pleasure from such events afterward is not so much a benign reflection of the crime as it is an extension of it. At the historical level, many of these artists often find that the aesthetic, religious, and political linking of destruction and redemption may actually have justified such terror in the killers' minds; what Saul Friedlander has called the redemptive anti-Semitism practised by the Nazis.

In contrast, Whiteread, Boltanski, Ullman, Hoheisel, and other artists of their generation propose memorial forms that refuse to domesticate the memory of the Holocaust, which do not make us at home with such memory, and never bring the events themselves into the reassuring house of redemptory meaning. They choose instead to leave such events unredeemable yet still memorable, unjustifiable yet still graspable in their causes and effects.

If 'estrangement from the world is a moment of art', as Adorno would have it, after Freud, then we might say that the uncanniness of a sculpture like Whiteread's crystallizes this moment of art.[8] But if the 'uncanny is uncanny only because it is secretly all too familiar, which is why it is repressed',[9] as Freud himself would have it, then perhaps no better term describes the condition of a contemporary Austrian culture coming to terms with the self-inflicted void of its lost and murdered Jews at its centre – a terrible void that is at once all too secretly familiar and unrecognizable, a void that at once defines a national identity, even as it threatens such identity with its own implosion.

CHAPTER 9

LESSONS FROM WHAT'S POOR

Monument and the Space of Power

CHRIS TOWNSEND

'It is remarkable how some people are able to put their opinions in lapidary form.'

Evelyn Waugh, *Brideshead Revisited*

Who now remembers William IV?

I ask because it was 'his' plinth at the north western corner of Trafalgar Square that, between June and November 2001, was occupied by Rachel Whiteread's *Monument* (45, 49). I ask because whilst the plinth was intended for the monarch's monument, at his death William had not left sufficient funds for its creation or erection. No statue of this minor sovereign, 1765–1837, ever found its way onto the platform intended to emphasize and elevate his majesty. The enduring mark of William IV's presence is, as it were, his absence; the lingering trace of his rule the largely unremarked vacancy on top of a granite pedestal; 'his' plinth until recently a vantage point for the pigeons for which Trafalgar Square is so internationally renowned, and the tribute to the monarchy an accumulating, and regularly scraped, layer of avian excrement.[1]

Trafalgar Square is, of course, famous for so much else besides the excreta of birds: it is a site of national monuments, and thus of a form of national memory. At the other corners of the square are, on the south side, statues of two generals of Britain's imperial history – Sir Henry Havelock, 1795–1857 (46), most famous for his suppression of the Indian Mutiny in 1857, and Sir Charles James Napier, 1782–1853, renowned for his largely peaceful quelling of Chartist unrest in 1839–41, and who later gave invaluable service to the nation through his conquest of the hill-tribes of

45   *Monument* 2001, resin and granite, 900 x 510 x 240cm (354 x 201 x 95in)

Sind; at the north eastern corner is Sir Francis Chantrey's statue of George IV, 1762–1830, erected in 1843. At the heart of the square, planned by John Nash in the 1820s and '30s as a foreground to William Wilkins's new National Gallery, and finally laid out by Sir Charles Barry in the 1840s, are two fountains installed in 1845, their basins remodelled by Sir Edwin Lutyens in 1939 to commemorate Admirals Sir David Beatty and Sir John Jellicoe, 1871–1935 and 1859–1935 respectively: two of the foremost naval commanders during the First World War.[2] The pools themselves were further decorated by Sir Charles Wheeler and William McMillan with bronze dolphins, mermen and mermaids. In 1966 a bust of Earl Cunningham of Hyndehope, 1883–1963, a naval commander of the Second World War, was installed alongside Lutyens's designs. Seemingly guarding the square are four lions, designed by Sir Edwin Landseer, and cast in bronze by Marochetti, installed in 1867. The most prominent, and famous, of Trafalgar Square's memorials, however, is Thomas Railton's Nelson Monument of 1843, a 145' column of granite topped with a 17' stone figure sculpted by Edmund Hodges Baily, commemorating Admiral Horatio Nelson, 1758–1805. The square itself is named after the admiral's posthumous victory over the French; a triumph which was understood to have permanently removed the threat of invasion by the armies of Napoleon.

Although planned as a cohesive site by Nash, and clearly a space in which the successes of monarchy and military are both remembered and celebrated, we might note that the expression of authority and service through sculpture and architecture within Trafalgar Square is decidedly piecemeal. With its central location and its imagination as a planned space Trafalgar Square might be understood as structuring the city through a rather late spatial manifestation of what Michel Foucault saw as 'models for the governmental rationality that was to apply to the whole of the territory.'[3] There is, however, no once-for-all announcement of imperial achievement or state power: rather, the design is added to gradually over more than a century, without necessarily too much thought being given to the modification of a grand plan.[4] Apart from the Nelson Monument and the salvaged and repositioned equestrian statue of Charles I, to the south of the square, and including Hammo Thorneycroft's 1886 statue of General George Gordon (relocated away from the square in 1943), all of the memorials are to individuals who died after the square was planned or created. The mounting of monuments reflects not so much any sense of the British past as it does an investment in the achievements of the recently dead, and undertakes that role for sculpture, identified by Rosalind Krauss, of projecting the isolated historical moment, in its immediate meaning, into the future.[5]

That is, Trafalgar Square, in its evolution as a space of monumental memory, rather than restoring already mythified historical moments to public attention within a rational structure, traces and keeps visible the *lived* experience of British military power and government through the nineteenth and into the twentieth century. But rather than combining these monuments to declaim a homogenous discourse of power, the differing histories of the statues of Havelock and Napier, for example, suggest that even in its commemoration of imperial prowess, Trafalgar Square is a site of continuously modified announcement by differing authorities. The nature of what is 'announced' – in its architecture and its monuments – and indeed the public understanding of them, is forever contingent upon events rather than on a singular and stable conception of national history and identity. In a typically British fashion, this most visible space of national memorial is organized by expediency. It is this being a response to lived experience, rather than being a constitution of space to accord with a more distanced perspective of historical circumstance and relevance, that makes Trafalgar Square into a kind of monumental manifestation of what we might otherwise shelter in the unconscious. And it is a space – much like that model of the memory developed by Freud with his paradigm of the *wunderblock* – that is subject to continual rewritings and erasures.[6] It is a space where signs jostle for attention, where signs – no matter that they are understood to be permanent – are continually displaced and placed in new contexts by the accumulation of new signs, new memories.

Whilst Havelock's monument was almost immediately sanctioned by the government of the day in response to a memorial fund begun in March 1858, Napier's death had gone with relatively little remark. Although one of two statues of the general by George Adams had been accommodated in St. Paul's Cathedral, the other looked likely to be situated in an out of the way square in Chelsea until Lord

46   Sculpture of Sir Henry Havelock by William Behnes, 1861, bronze

Elleborough – who as Governor General of India had benefited substantially from Napier's conquest of Sind – proposed its installation in the square in 1856. In the later years of the nineteenth century Havelock's reputation was sustained by his promotion as an exemplar of Christian virtue and imperial service, fuelled particularly by the general's evangelical profession.[7] Napier, by contrast, was perceived as endorsing the extension of suffrage espoused by Chartism and other movements, even if he did not condone the violent revolts favoured by some militants. Even as a general in the Indian Army he had correctly identified and endeavoured to correct some of the sources of discontent that would lead to the mutiny so brutally suppressed by Havelock. Napier was thus a rather unusual representative of the nineteenth century establishment to be commemorated in this square.[8]

As it became Britain's most favoured space of public protest and celebration, Trafalgar Square witnessed a contrast between temporary assembly and permanent installation: a more vigorous contestation of discourse than the discreet negotiations over the prominence of statuary effected within the British establishment. If it was, simply in its grand design, a space that announced the rational practice of state power, it immediately, as a sign of that power, solicited manifestations of resistance. The Chartist demonstration of 1848 began in the square, so too a wave of socialist rallies in the late 1880s, and significant Suffragette demonstrations in 1906 and 1908. In the 1930s Mosley's British Union of Fascists made use of the space. Public protest began in the square in the 1840s before it was finished (if indeed, with its vacant plinth and history of modification we can even now regard it as *finished*). As it became a place of protest, so the square also became used as a place of spontaneous popular celebration, at first to celebrate state occasions such as the Diamond Jubilee of Queen Victoria in 1895, then military victories such as the relief of Mafeking in 1900 and the ending of the Second World War. More routinely, Trafalgar Square became known as the focal point for New Year's Eve gatherings in London, with inebriated revellers cavorting in the pools of the fountains.

It was into this space, contested between public assemblage (characterized by the ludic, by temporary, more or less democratically minded, and arbitrary conjunction) and establishment sculpture and architecture (cohesive, designed, aesthetically conservative – if oversized – and meditated) that Whiteread's *Monument* was inserted. *Monument* was installed on one of two pedestals included in Barry's original layout. (The two southerly pedestals, now occupied by Napier and Havelock, were added for the installation of their statues in the 1850s.) Cast in two parts at Mike Smith's studios, in Crystal Clear 207 resin specially formulated for the work, *Monument* was, like the public assemblies in the square, a strictly temporary event. Nor was it the first object to occupy the vacancy created by William IV's neglect. As part of a project conceived by the Royal Society of Arts (R.S.A.), William's pedestal had been occupied first by Mark Wallinger's *Ecce Homo*, 1999, installed in July of that year, and then in March 2000 by Bill Woodrow's *Regardless of History*, 1999. Whiteread had been invited in 1998 to contribute to what became a highly publicized project, and in part conceived the work as 'a monument to the plinth.'[9] Whiteread intervened in a space dedicated to monumental commemoration at the heart of the British establishment. However, she also intervened in a contested space; albeit one in which the nature of the contestation was ephemeral and uneven, and in a culture in which commemoration itself had become a problematic issue. With the exception of Churchill's statue, establishment figures since the Second World War have tended to be effaced rather than commemorated; much as the power that they have nonetheless continued to embody and enact has been dispersed within institutions. If, at the beginning of a new century, the effecting of power is largely dematerialized into transparent and intangible institutions, so too is its representation – the archived sound-bite substituting for the monument – into forms that do not so readily provoke resistance, into motifs that cannot, unlike a statue, be readily toppled or defaced.[10]

179

Of course, being installed in Trafalgar Square, and thus accorded a prominence unusual for contemporary art in the public domain in Britain – even in the era of the YBAs, where visibility was more commonly effected in the pages of national newspapers – meant a concomitant insertion into political discourse. *Monument* was unveiled by Culture Secretary Chris Smith, whose address framed the work in terms of both an opening up of access to the arts (reflecting a longstanding commitment in British political life to the Arnoldian tradition of moral improvement through culture) and a notion of anti-elitism that seemed to equate 'difficulty' in art – that is the solicitation of intellectually demanding and perhaps contestatory interpretations by the art-work – with impulses that were fundamentally anti-democratic. This melding created a not-readily resolved tension between aspirations founded largely on the demands made by the artwork, and an imagination of the artwork as both easy on the eye and undemanding of the intellect. Smith's speech might have better been made in front of one of the older, lifelike statues – their meanings at the moment of installation obvious, even if their full historical resonance had since largely disappeared beneath a horizon of public ignorance and become contested through the rereading of Victorian history. What Derrida says of the naturalness of architecture in general – that 'It goes right through us to the point that we forget its very historicity... It is common sense itself'[11] – might be applied specifically both to our experience of Trafalgar Square and to Smith's expectation of the work's common sense rendering of meaning. But, like most of Whiteread's work, her installation in Trafalgar Square was difficult, required thought and imagination of its spectators, and solicited complex layers of interpretation. This difficulty, however, does not somehow make the work elitist, nor anti-democratic. The Minister's first mistake was to conflate facility with egalitarianism; his second to read *Monument* as if it were transparent.

Which of course it was: on a good day sunlight passing through the clear resin of the piece seemed to dissolve it into the traffic fumes. At other times and other angles of light, its reflections made it shimmer. At no point or moment was *Monument* visually stable. In this it was unlike any other monument in the square, and indeed the work's transparency and lightness seemed to mock the stolid obviousness of Victorian statuary. It was those works that reflected an anti-democratic instinct; that indeed celebrated and invoked national and imperial repression – even when used as platforms by protestors, the pissed, or more usually a combination of both; that most clearly communicated specific values and sentiments; that were in their obviousness anti-elitist, even as their legibility commemorated the elites that raised them; that were in the solidity of their marble, granite and bronze, *transparent* in their meaning. Though radically different in their appearance, all three sculptures installed on the plinth under the aegis of the R.S.A shared a number of common characteristics. They emphasized the scale of the other monuments in the square; they drew attention to the difference between that scale and the human; and in temporarily measuring that difference they made apparent the acts of elevation and installation, and the condition of permanence, as not natural but rather as ideologically inflected phenomena. *Monument*, as a monument to the plinth, drew attention to the realization of ideology through aesthetics, but it did so partly by remarking on the dematerialization of that ideology into naturalness (the way in which it 'passes through us'), and into *transparency* (the common-sense of representation).

As a Whiteread sculpture, *Monument* was unusual: most of the artist's works had relied upon casting interior volumes of objects that possessed or established that volume as a condition of their function. Space, or the possibility of space in the case of *Water Tower*, for example, was phenomenologically necessary to the object. Absence made the object and it also made possible a central thrust of the artist's work – the drawing of attention to the meanings of that absence. Whiteread's larger scale works before 2001 had necessitated the destruction or removal of the object in order to reveal her solidifying of interior volume. *Monument* is not a cast of the interior volume of Barry's plinth: it exactly replicates the external dimensions and decoration of its subject.[12] Spatially, it is a simulacrum of the object, and in some respects constitutes a return to those early casts, for example of the voids within baths, which clearly signal the objects that have shaped the spaces in which the artist is so interested. We might also understand *Monument* as a scaling up of concerns previously undertaken with smaller forms: in this way it perhaps resembles the ratio of *House* to *Ghost*, and represents a similar use of volume to rupture the meniscus of the public sphere. Between 1995 and 1998 Whiteread had produced a number of casts of plinths, including *Untitled (Rubber Plinth)*, 1996 (47), and *Untitled (Elongated Plinths)*, 1998 (48). As sculptural form *Monument* was a technical development of these pieces, albeit a question of casting technique in resin elevated to the highest level of difficulty. As a sculptural form in a public space the work raised a similar set of complex questions about history.

181

47 *Untitled (Rubber Plinth)* 1996, rubber, polystyrene 68.5 x 76 x 86.5cm
(27$^{1}/_{8}$ x 29$^{7}/_{8}$ x 34$^{1}/_{4}$in)

48 *Untitled (Elongated Plinths)* 1998, plastic and urethane foam (three elements)
each: 67.3 x 77.2 x 221cm (26³/₄ x 30¹/₄ x 87in)
overall dimensions: 67.3 x 376.6 x 221cm (26³/₄ x 148³/₈ x 87in)

Monument's creation did not necessitate the destruction of the original plinth: rather it used it as an integral part of the installation.[13] That installation does, however, require an absence in order to be effective, and effected: that is the absence of monumental sculpture. Absence is not a phenomenological necessity to the existence of a sculptural plinth. Rather – in order to be properly understood as plinth, as a bearer of communication – this object needs to carry another object, of a particular kind. Rather than being part of a play of presence and absence, in which each sustains the other, a plinth is conditioned by another presence. We do not recognize a sculptural plinth through its conjunction with something that is 'not plinth': as a sign a sculptural plinth both directs our gaze, and is understood as a functional object, through the presence of another sign – the sculpture. At the same time however, the act of pointing, the announcement of monumentality, is an act of erasure. We look at what is on top of the plinth: if we engage at all with the statuary's support it is for advice on exactly who we are looking at.

184

In this sense too Whiteread's originary subject was unusual. Her treatment of it, however, had something in common with *House*, with *Ghost*, with *Water Tower*. The failure of William IV to fund his memorial allowed Whiteread to emphasize the way in which the heightened visibility of monumental sculpture turns presence into absence – erasing, as it were, in the movement between signifiers, the support of one that holds the other in place – and to draw attention to the way in which this assumed invisibility of stone parallels an invisibility assumed by institutional structures. *Monument*, like much of Whiteread's other work, solidifies and manifests what is concealed; but what is solidified and manifested here is not space, however charged by memory and history, but the operations of memory and history concealed within, and rendered invisible by, a tangible, visible, object. *Monument* is in part about the language of sculpture: about the way in which the plinth as sign is understood only as functional object rather than as a sign invested with its own specific meanings and structure. After all, this particular plinth both preceded its erstwhile regal occupant, and, like its pair in the north eastern corner, was not intended to bear any specific statue, but rather one that would come after it. But in revealing the reduction of meaning to function, to bearer of the sign, Whiteread provided both an analysis of the rhetoric of power as it is manifested in sculptures, and of the character of institutional forces in an age when they more effectively rationalize and suborn their subjects through invisible agency or temporary tropes. She did so by turning the sign carried by the plinth into its obvious negative; by repeating the sign that is merely the harbinger of a sign as its own inversion; by emphasizing simultaneously the absence of a sculpture as sign and the elision of the sign beneath it; and by making it seem as if all that was solid had indeed melted into air.

Where Barry's plinth was all granitic substance, its echo, *Monument*, was, even if it weighed 11.3 tonnes, seemingly ephemeral. Certainly *Monument* wasn't there for good, but there were times when it seemed as though it wasn't there at all. Where the plinth was constructed in harmonious design ready to bear its sculpture, *Monument*, at times like ice, at times little more than a hazy condensation of the atmosphere, appeared so insubstantial that it could take no load. The sculpture that *Monument* bore lay beneath it: the plinth. Whilst it perhaps symbolized 'the world turned upside down' so fervently yearned for by every plebeian interloper who had used this patrician platform as soap-box, Whiteread's inversion of her subject meant that rather than functioning as a sign carried by the plinth, it pointed back towards the structure that carried it. In its evanescence and inversion *Monument* threw attention back onto the relationship between architecture and statuary, onto their functions, and onto the existence of that which is so readily overlooked.

As symbol, therefore, *Monument might* be understood as a remarkably democratic, even utopian, sculpture – and it was perhaps this that Chris Smith *really* wanted to say. Where stone architecture and bronze statuary evokes a particular understanding of the British establishment, Whiteread's piece looked like the work of a new age. Against impenetrability: transparency; against weight and mass: lightness; against the old hierarchical order of things: inversion; against the figuring of imperial violence: an abstract, airy, symbol; even, against something as old as stone: high-tech resin – past versus future. That is perhaps why Smith liked *Monument* so much: the work *could* be understood as embodying (or rather disembodying) all those values that were seemingly promulgated by his political party

49 *Monument* 2001

(New Labour) in its promises of modernization, accessibility, and cultural diversity. Even though it provided an effective historical commentary on the disembodiment of an authority far more dedicated to the disciplining of subjects than any Victorian general, with the right eyes and a properly worded press release *Monument* could instead be understood and explained as a symbol of the new order, replacing not the void allowed by William IV's neglect but rather a monument toppled in a revolutionary moment.

As work of art, however, *Monument* represented a complex negotiation of issues of language and the forms of art: that is of both what is represented, and how it is represented. In its shimmer *Monument* perhaps concealed what are charged subjects – the ideology of representation, the history of monuments – behind the screen of 'beauty'. And of necessity – in a society where engagement with art is attenuated by a combination of *recherché* connoisseural criticism in newspapers and not-wholly-ironic self-deprecation by young artists, and vilified as elitist by those politicos and cultural theorists who see art's chief function as the pacification of the subject – no one much talked about Whiteread's formal exercises, far less the critiques of ideology and art history which they embodied. All of the other monuments in Trafalgar Square, including those made in the twentieth century, are not terribly satisfying manifestations of neo-classical, nineteenth century sculpture: all conform to certain governing principles, vital amongst which are ideas of rationality and transcendence. By this I mean that they adhere to a linear model of temporality in which meaning unfolds (both in the short-term experience of the individual viewer, and more significantly in the unfolding of the purposes of a superior governing agency – whether god or 'the nation' – by whom the earthly powers manifested in monumental sculpture are authorized). As Rosalind Krauss puts it, for nineteenth century artists:

187

> time was the medium through which the logic of social and moral institutions revealed itself – hence the exalted position they gave to history painting as genre and to historical monuments. History was understood to be a kind of narrative, involving the progression of a set of significances that mutually reinforce and explicate each other,

and that seem driven as if by a divine mechanism toward a conclu-sion, toward the meaning of an event.[14]

Transcendence is thus a function of monumentality: the commemorated sub-ject endures beyond his historical moment, and in commemoration establishes that moment within a continuum that projects across time towards a more signifi-cant goal. Transcendence also functions in the experience of the viewer in relation to the monument: this is, as Krauss puts it, transcendence 'over the partial infor-mation that a single aspect of a figure can convey.'[15] It is knowledge granted to the viewer 'that, in some sense, enables one to see the object from everywhere at once, to *understand* the object even while seeing it.'[16] This operation is ideological rather than a natural consequence of perception. According to this principle, monuments are wholly and immediately legible: they do not solicit interpretation; and they interpolate their viewers into a given historical trajectory that, whilst it may be agreed between artist and subject, is elided from its wider audience by the sleight of mimesis, the scale of representation, and the schema of narrative.

Whiteread's *Monument* is, by contrast, nothing if not self-referential: it is a monument to monuments. But it is a work that, in its mimesis, discloses the inter-nal ideological structuring of the plinth. Of her use of clear resin in an earlier piece (at Documenta in 1992), Whiteread remarked, 'I wanted to make a work that had an inherent transparency so that its internal as well as its external structure could be revealed.'[17] *Monument* is a commentary upon the unseen: the unseen statue of William IV, certainly; on the ideological operations that demand and commission public statuary; but at the same time it is a reflection upon the attempt at visual tran-scendence made by such statuary. In this repetition and self-reference, Whiteread seemingly reiterates the challenge to the principles of rationality and transcendence in sculpture which Krauss sees as presented by Rodin at the end of the nineteenth century. Fundamental to Rodin's project is the goal of ridding sculpture of the mon-umental plinth.[18] *Monument's* self-reference, far from creating a work as transparent in meaning as it is in material, uses its lack of artifice to obfuscate the principles of monumental art on which it quite literally rests. Rather than participate in an agreed discourse whereby the plinth announces obvious meaning within a temporal progression, *Monument* frustrates that activity by foreclosing progress. Indeed, one could see the transparency of Whiteread's half of the equation as mirroring into the past everything that the monumental plinth is designed to project into the future. Somewhere along the dividing line between stone and resin is an arrest of time and its reversal.[19] This mirroring is not only temporal but spatial; indeed, as mirror *Monument* invokes Foucault's notion of the heterotopic space that in relation to other sites neutralizes or inverts 'the set of relations that they happen to designate, mirror or reflect.'[20] A similar antagonism is enacted against transcendence in *Monument's* transparency: never the same piece from day to day or indeed from one viewpoint to another because of its behaviour in light, the work did not readily permit visibility or immediate understanding, which a hierarchical reading of the piece, from the plinth upwards, should have facilitated. Paradoxically, *Monument's* total visibility rendered it intractable. Where the illusion of the transcendent individual, for the viewer, is promised by relief or dimension in the traditional materials of monumental sculpture, in *Monument* the ability to see everything, whether from outside or inside, means that one simultaneously witnesses the paradox of ideological disclosure in the age of democratic institutions: that seeing what is obvious, one sees nothing; that, whilst experiencing the disciplinary effects of those institutions, one no longer has their physical manifestation against which to protest.

Where Rodin undertakes his critique of monumental sculpture through repetition and opacity, and through radical but nonetheless recognizable modifications of and breaks with the aesthetic traditions in which he is grounded, Whiteread effects her project through repetition and transparency. Not incidentally, she too establishes modifications of and breaks with the aesthetic traditions in which she is grounded – particularly those of minimalism and postminimalism. It is the difference between those aesthetic traditions – representation versus non-representation – that elides the common intent. And yet, of course, Whiteread's sculpture goes beyond representation: rather than abstracted non-representation, it is facsimile, a displacement of the real into another medium that nonetheless shares and extends the space of what it mimes. This strategy parallels typical postminimal activity – I am thinking in particular of a work such as Michelle Stuart's *East/West Wall*

Memory Relocated, 1976, in the 'Rooms' exhibition at PS1, where the artist:

> took enormous rubbings [*in pencil on muslin backed paper*] of two
> facing walls of a corridor, picking up cracks, peels, wainscoting
> and an old bulletin board. These she transposed, hanging each on
> the opposite wall from which it was made, thus reversing their
> locations, but maintaining their relative positions. Like fossils they
> recorded the archaeology of their past.[21]

Unlike Stuart, however, or Richard Serra in a work such as *Casting*, 1969,[22] with both of whom she might be understood to share a thematic, Whiteread's *formal* exploration of monumentality and representation is conducted here through a reprise of the strategies of modernist sculpture that emerged in the wake of Rodin. The brilliance of Whiteread's piece is the way in which it uses those explorations to develop a historically informed commentary on the ideology of the monument, and in particular uses its transparency (its 'beauty') to both embed and elide that critique on the function of art in the public sphere, within the public sphere.

Monument plays not only in the nebulous bounds of postmodernity but in a better defined modernist terrain that, following Krauss, we might here triangulate between Tatlin, Boccioni and Naum Gabo. Boccioni's project is a radical analysis of sculpture, applying the lessons that Cubism had worked through in the pictural field, including the rupturing of that field with collage and assemblage, to the sculptural. Like monumental sculpture, however, Boccioni's work is idealist, directed towards the 'revelation of a transcendent reality, rather than the manifestation of a factual reality.'[23] The idea of 'relative motion', of seeking to both manifest and stabilize the viewer's shifting perceptions of the object in space, that Boccioni first propounds in *Development of a Bottle in Space*, 1912 (50), might seem to undermine the monument's blunt assertion of historical presence. However, idealism resurfaces here not obviously in the monument's activity of imposing a historical moment on the future, but in what Krauss identifies as an attempt to transcend 'the poverty of partial vision.'[24] In attempting total intelligibility of the object – which we need to keep distinguished from the indexical properties of the facsimile, since an exact image does not equate to an exact understanding – Boccioni 'segregated his *Bottle*

50   Umberto Boccioni *Development of a Bottle in Space* 1912, bronze
38.1cm (15in) height

from real space – from the world in which we actually move – to install it firmly within something that can only be characterized as conceptual space.'[25] In making *Monument*, Whiteread seems to me to be interested in something like 'relative motion', although the 'motion' with which she is concerned is not the shifting of viewpoints, but the shifting of signs, both in space and across time, that constitutes history. Where Boccioni attempted to symbolize that motion within the stable object, Whiteread enacted it in the instability of the object, the refusal of *Monument* to establish itself as a distinct entity indifferent to the conditions in which it was viewed. The conundrum of *Monument* was not simply that you could move around it, but that it seemed to move around on you.

What facilitated this instability – within what was, apparently, straightforward facsimile – was the work's transparency. What trumped the idealism of the monumental was the condition that you could see through history. Where Boccioni 'cast a meditation on the conceptual transparency of a bottle in solid bronze'[26] Whiteread cast a meditation on the conceptual solidity of the monument (and all it represents) in something that was near totally transparent. In the 1920s Gabo had moved from a conceptual transparency in his exposure of 'the core of the geometric object'[27] to an economy of invisibility, using clear plastics in small-scale assemblages. As Krauss suggests, 'the literal transparency of the intersecting vertical planes of a work such as the 1923 *Column* is merely the material analogue for the underlying idea of the construction: namely that one must have access to the core of the object where the principle of its structure – its rigidity and its coherence as a volume – is lodged in the intersection maintained along its axial center.'[28] At the heart of this project was an understanding of the object as occupying a particular, that is ideational, space, in which meaning can be simultaneously arrested and wholly apprehended. Both Boccioni and Gabo thus maintained the idealist insistence on the transcendence of sculptural and monumental forms – but they did so through an attempt to transfer this transcendence of form into a transcendence of the spectator by stabilizing and manifesting the totality of the form's rhetorical possibilities for analysis. (It is, if you like, the move from the authority of the text to the authority of the reader.)

With what looks like an informed perversity, Whiteread works through Boccioni's critique with the materials of Gabo (or rather with a technical apotheosis of materials to which Gabo might have aspired) to reach a position much like that of Tatlin; one that seeks to manifest the historical conditions of the object rather than its transcendence of history. The formal quest for the revelation of structure leads to the corresponding disclosure that the structure has no heart. But rather than transpose transcendent authority onto the viewer of the monument (Boccioni's ideal), Whiteread proposes a shared instability between spectator and statue: we are no more permanent either in the endurance of our affections or the ephemerality of our lives than are monuments stripped of their historical relation and the veil of power (which are those monuments, whether of Lenin, the Shah of Iran or Saddam Hussein, toppled by crowds.) Tatlin, of course, made manifest the continuum of natural and sculptural space. As Krauss argues, in his corner reliefs Tatlin used 'the real space of the room'[29] as an integral part of the construction, employing the tension between surfaces and objects to sustain the sculptural object. Where for Boccioni (and indeed for Gabo) the plinth continued to act parenthetically, separating out the sculptural statement as significant, for Tatlin at this point there was a bound relationship between the two terms. Significance, and the act of its signification, comes with a supporting apparatus, as *Monument* makes clear in its employment of the 'real spaces' of the plinth and of Trafalgar Square. This rehearsal of the dematerialization of the monument draws attention to the way in which modernism was, perhaps, ahead of its time: the process of elision prefaced and predicted the metaphoric dematerialization, within democracies at least, of the individuals whom monuments were meant to commemorate. With that rehearsal, however, comes a renewed critique of the monuments that are there, in this space of established authority. And there are further commentaries, registered in the formal conditions of *Monument* – its transparency, its visual instability – firstly on the way in which monumental power has preserved itself, generally intact, through rendering itself intangible and invisible within institutions and bureaucracies, and additionally on the related but ephemeral and uncommemorated contributions to democracy made within Trafalgar Square.

Monument embodies an appreciation of the implications of sculptural and monumental languages – their rhetorical forms – that, in its attention to the margins, to the invisible, the overlooked, and the supposedly natural and obvious – reconfigures the object itself to disclose those meanings which it bears but does not 'naturally' admit to us. By an attention to what is no more than a parenthesis to the monument – that which has no apparent value in itself, that which is invisible – Whiteread reveals the interdependence of signs and the sliding between signs in space across time: Trafalgar Square is not only a space for the exhibition of state power, it is a space, a heterotopia, which may temporarily act as a theatre of resistance or celebration for those who have little or no power. If it does anything, *Monument* tells us that there is no such thing as the natural or the stable in the domain of art's rhetoric. The plinth's gesture towards its crowning statue may also be a gesture of self-elision, but we cannot properly understand the historically embedded meanings of the monument unless we recognize how this conjuring trick is performed. The monument is a closure of meaning; in its 'common-sense' we understand everything, or think we do. As prefatory statement the plinth is forgotten in the completeness of all that we see. Whiteread recognizes that the failure of signification (here specific to the empty plinth, but universally a condition of the bounded object) is itself a signification. This concern is at the heart of her project, regardless of how the void that she apprehends is configured. Indeed, the sustained emotional force of much of Whiteread's large-scale sculpture suggests that that collapse of the sign (up to and including its disappearance) may be more charged with meaning than any comprehensive, transcendental statement. Language is necessarily incomplete, since, despite its yearning for totality of description and comprehension, it always anticipates a further comment, whether a supplement or a reply. As Jacques Lacan points out, the incomplete proposition produces an effect at the point where it no longer offers signs, and apparently there is no meaning.[30] What Lacan identifies is that rhetorical device known as *apopoesis*, the hesitation that suggests the speaker is so affected by his subject he is unable to proceed. The point at which signification is here effected is the very structural element (the ellipsis; the frame; the plinth) that guarantees incompleteness. What signifies at a certain moment is thus not the proposition, whether the content of the image, the text, the monument, or the deferred end of the proposition which the sign would seek to transcend, but that which guarantees the deferral. (Such an inhibition or deferral, of course, is not a loss of power, but rather an emphasis of power in the choice to be silent, before continuing to overwhelm one's audience.)

Whiteread's critique of Gabo and Boccioni – even as she pursues the total apprehension of structure espoused, in different ways, by both artists – is concentrated in a concern not with the statement of the object, but with the *non-statements* that define the object, the rhetorical silences of monumental, sculptural and architectural space. In *Monument* we have however, rather than the void, a reflection of an object that voids itself. By repeating and inverting that object which would be a space, (that sign which would be a non-sign, by, as it were, providing us with the closing parenthesis, so (...)), Whiteread makes the elision palpable. This is not, however, simply a formal exercise; rather (as is usual for Whiteread) it is a project that speaks to us as human beings caught up in our own lives and within history. Patrick Elliott has movingly commented on Whiteread's bonding of the ordinary human body to ordinary space; remarking of the early castings made beneath beds and baths, that 'These are the dumb, unchampioned cornerstones of life: not since Bonnard, Vuillard and Sickert has an artist moved them more effectively to centre stage.'[31] There is too, for all the rhetoric that has been declaimed within Trafalgar Square since the 1840s, a similar dumbness surrounding its monuments. It is not a place where the quotidian is given lasting voice. The angry and often ill-thought yells of Chartist protestor and poll-tax rioter, the carefully crafted speeches of trades union leaders and anti-war organizers, have all been ephemeral interventions in the space of monument and authority, even as they have contributed to the square's own dissident tradition. Even when misguided, violent, or merely vulgar, they were never dumb, those ordinary people, but quickly muted, however effective or justified their complaint against history, no matter how joyous their festivities. Trafalgar Square holds no monuments to champion the achievements of the Chartists or the Suffragettes, no sign that records how ordinary people celebrate national identity or even something as infuriatingly banal as a New Year. For a while it did, in

195

Monument. Cutting off monumental discourse at its preamble, *Monument* high-lighted the rhetorical strategies of authority, and in that space, that silence, we heard the voices which the statue on the plinth would mute. It was perhaps fitting that the work was removed, itself elided as the voices it commemorated were lost. In November 2001 the sculpture was taken to storage. At much the same time Ken Livingstone, the Mayor of London, announced the formation of the racily titled 'Fourth Plinth Commissioning Group' to make recommendations on future works to appear in *Monument*'s place. Whilst a project for another temporary installation is underway, three years on the plinth remains empty except for its carpet of spikes. Its reduction to bearer of deterrent is perhaps symbolic of the dilemmas of author-ity in post-Imperial Britain, unable any longer to sustain the kind of imagination that would authorize any articulation of power as visible, and easily targeted, as a monumental statue; but equally unprepared to grant a temporary platform to pests: whether anarchists or artists, pigeons, revellers or rioters.

CHAPTER 10

LIVE AS IF SOMEONE IS ALWAYS WATCHING YOU

George Orwell's, Rachel Whiteread's
and the BBC's versions of *Room 101*

CHRIS TOWNSEND

Everyone carries a room inside them.

Franz Kafka

In 2003, as part of the BBC's 'Broadcasting House Public Art Programme', Rachel Whiteread was invited to devise a project that employed one of the rooms within Broadcasting House.[1] The chosen space was Room 101, the office used by the writer George Orwell when he worked for the BBC between 1940 and 1943, as a Talks Assistant, and later as a Producer, within its Eastern Service (Indian Section). As a result of an internal redesign of the building the room was to be demolished, and was thus eminently suited for the preservation of its interior space through casting in what has become Whiteread's 'signature' style.

The BBC's invitation to Whiteread produced a solidification of space that, as metaphor, seemed to sediment all of those intangible, abstract, ephemeral elements – speech, thought, memory, a critical imagination – that were Room 101's invisible residue, and indeed Orwell's legacy to English letters. But powerful though that activity is, and powerful though that yoking of the real space of Orwell's broadcasts to his commentary on totalitarianism might have been, any perspective granted by Whiteread's work, *if that were all its scope*, would have been largely retrospective. *1984*, as a novel written in 1948–49, was not a prophecy, but rather a commentary on Orwell's own times. By the end of the twentieth century the age of world-wide dominance for brutal totalitarian regimes seemed largely over. But Whiteread's *Room 101* is not, of course, simply a backward glance at a lost era of paternal (or fraternal) dictators, jack-booted secret-policemen and perpetual war. Like much of Whiteread's recent public art, *Room 101* addresses the present through both historical reflection – in this case on the BBC's relationship to Orwell – and a proleptic gaze into the future. What makes her casting so pertinent, then, is its mute witness simultaneously to those values of language and subjectivity cherished by Orwell, and to the radical changes in recent years to the tradition of public service broadcasting originally promulgated by the BBC in the 1920s. In particular we might see *Room 101* as encapsulating a particular conceptual and linguistic dilemma for the BBC that is hidden within the now clichéd promise of its first Director-General, J.C.W. Reith, to 'educate, inform and entertain'.[2] On the one hand there is a tradition of, and commitment to, presenting, or seeking, the truth in plain language; on the other there is a tradition of and commitment to mass entertainment. Reith, however, understood a very different meaning for 'entertainment' to that practised today within the BBC (and broadcast media in general): 'it [*entertainment*] may be part of a systematic and sustained endeavour to re-create, to build up knowledge, experience and character.'[3]

These days, in attempting to fulfil its Reithian prescription, the Corporation seems to make a dual and conflicting use of Orwellian concepts. I'd suggest that one way of understanding Whiteread's *Room 101* is to see it as reflecting the manner in which central themes of horror and human degradation in *1984* have become figures of fun, rearticulated for the purposes of entertaining an audience, not just by the BBC, but by broadcasters in general. In this case Whiteread's inversion of surface becomes a metaphor for inversion of values: a sign for the 'doublethink' that is now necessary within the BBC in order to relate the demands of the present moment to the traditions of public service broadcasting. Whiteread's work is *just* a cast of space, her motif: but in casting space it seems to me that Whiteread does not *merely* create an indexical sign of absence. In all her work she also creates a reflexive index of the historical context in which the absent object is situated. (Good examples here would be the inverted surfaces of *House* or the inverted orientation of *Monument*). *Room 101* is no different in this respect: looking at the work, in the disjunctive setting of the V&A, the critic cannot help but be drawn to a meditation on the BBC's relationship to George

51   *Untitled (Room 101)* 2003, mixed media, 300 x 500 x 643cm (118¹/₈ x 196³/₄ x 253¹/₈in)

Orwell's writing; but it seems to me unavoidable that such a meditation is itself metonymic of a larger issue – that of the relationship of broadcasting to subjectivity at the beginning of the twenty-first century. *Room 101* manages to simultaneously embody the *internal* dilemmas of the BBC and their *external* consequences.

Orwell used Room 101 to prepare and broadcast essays and discussions directed at the most unsettled of Britain's imperial possessions, during a period of historical crisis.[4] The space became better known, however, through its reincarnation as 'Room 101' in Orwell's final novel, *1984*. In that story of totalitarian power and the individual, 'Room 101' was a torture chamber; but it was one that – with an attention to individual subjectivity unusual for the agencies of terror, and therefore all the more sadistic for that – customized its traumas according to the personal habits and phobias of its victims. *1984* was equally notable for the way in which Orwell emphasized the use of language by authoritarian governments, distorting the historical truth that plain speaking should express, to justify their arbitrary and repressive actions. In *1984* history is endlessly rewritten to conform to the conditions of the present. In the course of this revision it also ceases to matter: in a sense there is no history, only an eternal present moment in which the vast majority of the population have no consciousness of time and events beyond their immediate purview. 'Nothing exists except an endless present in which the Party is always right.'[5]

However, in *1984* Orwell was not simply reacting to the regimes of the 1930s and '40s, but to the ideas expressed by the political philosopher James Burnham in *The Managerial Revolution*.[6] One of Orwell's central observations about Burnham's argument for the perpetuation of a planned, oligarchical society is that his brand of 'managerialism' responds pragmatically to historical circumstance in order to promote the greatest efficiency in social and economic behaviour and maintain power. Despite having established that Burnham's admiration of efficiency is flexible, shifting its object of valorization away from fascism or communism as a consequence of events, what Orwell overlooks is that the habit of supporting the dominant tendency, regardless of ethical considerations, will lead to 'managerial' democracy in the event of democracy's historical triumph.[7] Albeit that I'm co-opting Burnham's appellation as much as observing his ideas, I'd suggest that western societies since the mid-twentieth century have valued the efficient manager as a marker of social progress (rather as the jurist, the intellectual, the artist or even the politician were valued in earlier times) to such an extent that anyone succeeding under the rubric of those now obsolescent roles is little more than a species of manager (with Andy Warhol the finest exemplar of such behaviour in the arts.)[8] We live now in a democratic 'managerial' society (which might have surprised James Burnham less than it would have surprised and disappointed Orwell); and we live in a culture dominated by 'management speak'.

The misuse of communication within politics and public life was famously encapsulated in Orwell's neologisms 'doublethink' and 'newspeak': forms of language and thought in which one manages to say one thing whilst believing, and effecting, its opposite, or in which it ultimately becomes impossible to have dissenting thoughts because the words do not exist to articulate them. In order to promote a society that at least imagines and promotes itself as 'efficient' – even if in *1984* it patently isn't – it is necessary to disable the subjective capacity of individuals to think and speak for themselves, and thus dissent from the imagination of progress.

201

In *1984* Orwell describes a form of television – the 'telescreen' – from which streams martial music and the most banal and authoritarian propaganda; which carries crude disciplinary exercises; and which, unlike any form of the medium so far developed, allows someone else (in this case functionaries of the Thought Police) to watch and overhear its audience. That audience, however, is comparatively small, largely restricted to Party members. In Oceania the proles constitute some 85% of the state's population, but only a few of that bovine, disregarded mass have 'telescreens' in their homes.[9] What keeps the proles from rebelling, at least in the eyes of the dissident Winston Smith, is 'heavy physical work, the care of home and children, petty quarrels with neighbours, films, football, beer and above all gambling'.[10] To maintain this sedation, the Ministry of Truth, where Winston Smith works, has 'a whole chain of separate departments dealing with proletarian literature, music, drama and entertainment generally. Here were produced rubbishy newspapers containing almost nothing except sport, crime and astrology, sensational five-cent novelettes, films oozing with sex, and sentimental songs'.[11] As a separate and final form of distraction there is the Lottery. 'The Lottery, with its weekly pay-out of enormous prizes, was the one public event to which the proles paid serious attention. It was probable that there were some millions of proles for whom the Lottery was the principal, if not the only reason for remaining alive. It was their delight, their folly, their anodyne, their intellectual stimulant.'[12]

In writing *1984* Orwell had only a few years of experience of television to go on as a model for how 'telescreens' might be used. In September 1939, when the BBC's nascent service was suspended on the outbreak of war, there were only 23,000 licence holders in Britain.[13] The BBC's television broadcasts had run for just under three years. Clearly television was seen as a luxury that catered only to those people wealthy enough to buy a set. Even with the post-war resumption of broadcasting, during the years 1947–48, when Orwell was writing *1984*, there were only, at most, 45,564 holders of joint wireless and television licences.[14] Orwell could not be blamed for seeing television as a form of communication that, effectively, served the upper echelon of managers and the intelligentsia who effectively ran the country. (This, of course, was that social caste which Burnham imagined as the dominant force in managerially efficient totalitarian societies.) Even in 1951, a year after Orwell's death, there would be only 763,941 joint licence holders.[15] Of the television audience at the end of 1947, divided by social class, 48% belonged to 'Class I' – that is the managerial and 'upper' classes of British society; only 25% belonged to 'Class III'.[16] However, the number of viewers grew rapidly (exceeding two million by 1953) and the class bias of ownership within the audience changed accordingly.[17] Today less than one percent of the population does not have at least one television in their home. Television rapidly moved from being the not-so-mass medium of the managerial elite to become a ubiquitous phenomenon. Orwell might also have been aware of the interest of totalitarian states in television broadcasting, and he would certainly have known of the Nazis' enthusiasm for radio. Unlike Britain, Germany did not cease television broadcasts with the outbreak of war. The service was maintained until the destruction of the last transmitter at Witzleben in 1943, suggesting that the Nazis indeed saw television as a significant means of communication, rather than a luxury.[18]

For most of its viewers, television now, though not necessarily the BBC, is the principal source of entertainment, of information and of news. Deliberately, however, in this essay I'm restricting myself to the way that television has used, and uses, Orwellian concepts. In particular I want to show through three examples (Room 101; Big Brother; the Lottery) how central motifs within Orwell's dystopia have been inverted in a culture that simultaneously enacts its own forms of degradations upon the human subject whose celebration it so relentlessly mimes. I'm not suggesting that secret agencies of the state are watching the television audience through its sets, in order to control or at least spy upon dissident elements. Nor, more seriously, am I suggesting that television is the uncomplicated institution of social pacification imagined by Orwell, nor even 'simply' one of those apparatuses for the reproduction of ideas perceived by Louis Althusser, unconsciously dedicated simply to turning out compliant and efficient subjects.[19] Like most other institutions in democratic societies broadcasting is fissured by ideology in the same moment as it helps to constitute ideology for us. Nor do we live in Orwell's Oceania: Western societies are not largely composed of what that mythical agent of rebellion Emmanuel Goldstein in *1984* calls 'the great mass of human beings...normally stupefied by poverty'.[20]

What I do want to suggest, however, is that the linguistic corruption of totalitarian societies and Burnham's 'managerialism' that Orwell addressed in *1984* didn't go away with totalitarianism. Rather, a distinctive form of linguistic debasement emerged in democratic but 'managerial' societies as a consequence of their own uses of mass-media to 'educate, inform and entertain'. This attenuation of thought is equally pernicious in its disabling of individual subjectivities and the capacity for critical engagement with history. There are other forms of stupefaction at work beside poverty. It's been observed often enough that if Modernist models of a dystopian future are applied to our present circumstance, the one with the closest resemblance is Huxley's *Brave New World*, whose inhabitants are stupefied by erotics and by glut, rather than by terror and poverty as they are in *1984*. Clearly subordination to 'the meretricious effluvia of late capitalism'[21] is of a different order to the eternal 'boot in the face' promised to mankind by Winston Smith's torturer, O'Brien, but that effluvia nonetheless has consequences for the human subject, which include the erasure of history and historical consciousness. Appropriately enough, given Whiteread's rendering concrete of Orwell's room, we can see these processes of debasement and stupefaction at work in spatial terms; both in terms of the individual's critical consciousness in a private space and the promise made by the mass media in democratic societies of access to the public sphere.

'The worst thing in the world,' said O'Brien, 'varies from individual to individual. It may be burial alive, or death by fire, or by drowning, or by impalement, or fifty other deaths. There are cases where it is some quite trivial thing, not even fatal.'[22] Room 101 in the Ministry of Love contains no specific thing; interestingly it seems to be one of the few rooms in the building that does not contain a 'telescreen'. What is brought into it is the subject's worst nightmare; the room is a cipher for the capacity of torturers to commit upon you the worst atrocity you can imagine. But there is, perhaps, an even more paranoid aspect to the space. It is a room in which your tormentors reveal – as O'Brien does to Winston Smith – that they know your dreams; where it becomes clear that the most private space imaginable to the individual – private because it is not really a space, because it is not tangible – has been the subject of another's scrutiny.

What we have in Room 101 is the ultimate torture chamber, one that takes place inside the victim's head: possibly not the dream of every thug who extracts sadistic pleasure from the victim's body, but certainly that of the bureaucrats behind them; for Orwell, the party-disciplined 'intellectuals' and truth-extractors of Stalin's Soviet Union and Hitler's Germany. Despite the victory of democracy against totalitarian regimes in both World War Two and the 'cold war', those thugs and their directors did not vanish from the face of the earth. Indeed, there were moments in the 'cold war' and post-colonial liberation struggles and after, when such practices were sustained directly by democracies – whether in Algeria or Vietnam – or by their allies, satraps and surrogates – whether of the ilk of Saddam Hussein or Augusto Pinochet. Torture did not disappear, any more than totalitarian regimes. Room 101 as Orwell described it still has a very real existence throughout the world.

Room 101 has another existence in the BBC besides having been 'Orwell's room' (real space) in Broadcasting House. As *Room 101*, it is the title of a television programme, hosted by the comedian Paul Merton, in which various celebrities, known to the audience largely through their appearances on other television programmes, nominate their pet-hates for consignment, after brief, 'witty' and provocative debate, to the lumber room of phobia that Orwell's room (creative construct) has become in the popular imagination. Before Whiteread ever got around to metonymizing the complex relations of power and language that permeated Room 101 as both space and construct, the BBC itself, in its use of Orwell's concept had successfully debased them. *Room 101* (TV programme) took a representation of the horror of totalitarianism that might have had some effect upon the concerned critical reader of literature and reformulated it as entertainment for the uncritical viewer, pitched at a level that might have diverted Orwell's 'proles', had the party felt the need for them to have television as compensation for their suborned existence.

Room 101 has become a catchphrase: in the words of Vivien Lovell of Modus Operandi, the commissioning agency for Whiteread's project, the space 'stands as a metaphor in the collective memory and the popular imagination of the worst thing that can happen to you.'[23] Lovell is of course developing on O'Brien's succinct remark, 'The thing that is in Room 101 is the worst thing in the world.'[24] But between Orwell's novel, 1948, and Whiteread's cast, 2003, there seems to be a vast moral and conceptual chasm, despite the almost exact duplication of language used to describe the architectural space. We have moved from a scenario where rats may be allowed to gnaw the flesh from a man's cheekbones or his eyes from their sockets to one where comedians banter with each other over their allegedly phobic responses to, say, people from Wales, or the Ford Mondeo. If the things that are consigned to Room 101 by this process are indeed 'the worst...that can happen to you', and if we find that prospect entertaining, then there is, I'd suggest, a particular problem afflicting participants and viewers alike. That problem is the refusal to take history seriously. Indeed, it might be the refusal to even recognize that history exists, certainly in the way it is described by Orwell, and in the way in which the tortures he alludes to are still practised. What stood in the imagination as a sign for the inhuman degradation of fellow human subjects is now a source of harmless fun. This, perhaps, is the heart of the BBC's problem: if its audience knows of Room 101, they know of it through this programme, through entertainment. They do not know of it through Orwell, through education and enlightenment. If, as Michael Tracey observes, 'the idea of public service broadcasting rests on the mighty and worthy ambition that we can, collectively, be *better* than we are',[25] then something is seriously amiss, either with broadcast media seeking to educate, inform and entertain; with the educational and moral status of its audience, of which the perceived quality of broadcasting is sometimes understood to be an index, or, more likely, with the imbricated effects of each upon the other.

The BBC has not been alone in this process of trivializing Orwell, of course. One of the most successful programmes broadcast in Britain in the last decade has been *Big Brother* on Channel 4. Here members of the public, chosen from a large list of applicants, become brief, low-luminance celebrities through sharing each other's company in a house under the constant scrutiny of TV cameras. The audience votes each week to expel one of the competitors from the 'Big Brother House' on the criteria of their 'personality'; the survivor wins a large cash prize to the accompaniment of hysterical publicity in the tabloid newspapers. For the third series, in 2002, there were some 10,000 videoed applications to become a contestant. That series was covered by nightly live broadcasts on Channel 4, accompanied by a more or less continuous feed in the evenings on the channel's subscription E4 network, and wholly continuous feed on a website that attracted between 3.5 and 4.5 million 'hits' per day.[26] For Channel 4, originally conceived as a medium for more experimental, challenging productions that might only cater to a minority audience, the programme attracts one of its largest audiences.

The connection to *1984* is in the appropriation of Orwell's phrase 'Big Brother is watching you'. In Orwell's imagination of the totalitarian state 'Big Brother' was the party leader whose face appeared on posters on every wall, posters 'so contrived that the eyes follow you about when you move.'[27] Although with his 'heavy black moustache and ruggedly handsome features'[28] Orwell's dictator seems to be based on Stalin, Big Brother serves as an archetype of the apparently benevolent national leader, who nonetheless scrutinizes every move of his people and punishes with torture and obliteration (from life and the historical record) those who dissent. Ultimately it is not even necessary for Big Brother to exist as a real human being: he is 'the embodiment of the party' who can never die.[29] Again we begin with a concept that is truly horrifying: the eternal, all-seeing patriarch, who represents a political system that perpetuates its rule through the brutal stifling of disagreement and the constant revision of history. Big Brother represents an ahistorical world, one in which it no longer matters *what* happened. With the inversion of the idea from one of horror to one of entertainment we end with the reduction of the television audience to voyeurs, vaguely hoping that two (or more) of the programme's excruciatingly banal participants might end up having sex or fighting.

The National Lottery was instituted in the United Kingdom in 1994 as a means of raising money to support what the government saw as 'good causes'. Whilst policy responsibility for the Lottery resides with the Department of Culture, Media and Sport, the 'competition' itself is run as a commercial enterprise by Camelot plc. From the very beginning of the scheme, the BBC participated, broadcasting live the random selection of lottery numbers as the centrepiece of a Saturday night light-entertainment programme. Although the substantial numbers of viewers of and participants in the Lottery have waned since 1994, the game remains a valuable source of income to a government department responsible for areas of public life (in particular 'culture') that were the subject of savage cutbacks in expenditure throughout the 1980s. Lottery funds have made possible a number of major projects within British public life that would otherwise have been impossible. It is worth observing, however, that those projects only became *impossible* because of an increasing emphasis within government on cutting public spending, on culture in particular, from tax revenues. Such otherwise frivolous expenditure can only be justified, it seems, if the source of revenue is a voluntary tax, rather than one levied by central government.

The BBC's coverage of the Lottery undoubtedly fostered the widespread national interest in the game. Public enthusiasm meant that the Lottery draw drew a substantial audience, eager to see if they were lucky enough to have won. Despite the

207

decline in the number of players, in 2002 the BBC signed an agreement with Camelot plc, guaranteeing coverage of the draw for another four years. In the words of Jana Bennett, BBC Director of Television, the agreement 'allows BBC ONE to offer more new and entertaining programming for our audiences...and builds on the success of our current Lottery shows which audiences are clearly enjoying.'[30] Rather like the distribution of television sets in the post-war era, there was initially a distinct class bias amongst Lottery players. However, there has been no rapid evening out or reversal of this bias with the passing of time. This is principally because most Lottery players already belong to Classes II and III (in the crude terms of B.P. Emmett's early analysis of television viewers). Effectively it is the poorer elements of society who choose to buy tickets; those for whom poverty may not be stupefying, but for whom the winning ticket nonetheless promises a life where you don't worry daily about how to pay the bills. The draw may be the one public event to which ticket holders pay serious attention. It *is* 'their delight, their folly, their anodyne, their intellectual stimulant.'

We can't, of course, equate the Lottery audience with Orwell's proles: or can we? Orwell, after all, was basing 'the proles' in *1984* on his observations of working class life as he saw it in the 1930s and '40s and indeed romanticized it – as only an Old Etonian could – in his essay 'The English People'. The BBC's Lottery Draw audience is clearly not 'stupefied by poverty', but equally it is neither so critically judicious, nor so prosperous, as to recognize that odds of 14,000,000 to one don't offer much prospect of a return. In the name of mass-entertainment the BBC continues to promote this Orwellian distraction for the ordinary people of Britain. As Orwell remarked of 'the English masses' resistance to what might be taken as disdain for 'harmless fun', 'they seem to be winning their battle against the kill-joy minorities.'[31] But in writing *1984* only three years later Orwell had clearly come to see the 'harmless fun' of state promoted games of chance as another means of sedating a population in whom otherwise there might lie hope of social change. By the time that Whiteread comes to make her reflection on Orwell, the BBC is happily engaged in the transmission of that particular sedative at the same time as it is administering a once terrifying Orwellian concept as entertainment. Quite what it is that is being sedated – perhaps the development of independent critical faculties, rather than the revolutionary spirit yearned for by Winston Smith – remains open to question. Like Winston, one is not drawn to question how, but merely why.

I have of course been grotesquely unfair to the BBC and to television in general in the above examples. At the same time as it has made Room 101 into a figure of fun, and participated in the anodyne that is the National Lottery, the BBC has made a number of programmes designed to educate and inform its audience about George Orwell and his work. That tradition stretches back to a live dramatization for television of *1984* as early as 1954, which attracted a large audience.[32] The corporation did, after all, commission Rachel Whiteread to make an artwork of the room where Orwell worked. The BBC is still capable of self-reflection. That earnest endeavour is the other part of the BBC's remit: juxtaposing notions of informing and educating with the meretricious nonsense of the Lottery as 'entertainment' and a comedy programme, and with Channel 4's *Big Brother*, we get a sense of the dilemma faced by public service broadcasting. (And we should perhaps include Channel 4 under that rubric, given the original terms of its charter and given that it is as likely, perhaps more likely, to produce a worthwhile, intelligent film about a writer like Orwell, even if it is busy debasing his ideas elsewhere in the schedules.)

It's easy to cite a critic such as Jürgen Habermas here, to bemoan the decline of critical values in culture as a consequence of mass-mediation:

> Mass culture has earned its rather dubious name precisely by achieving increased sales by adapting to the need for relaxation and entertainment on the part of consumer strata with relatively little education, rather than through the guidance of an enlarged public toward the appreciation of a culture undamaged in its substance.[33]

Habermas tends to get a bad press these days for his bourgeois nostalgia. But it was that guidance of an enlarged public *towards an undamaged culture* that was at the heart of the BBC's agenda from its incorporation, and despite the vicissitudes of recent history I'd guess that it would still be a maxim close to the corporation's collective heart. That the BBC audience's familiarity with Room 101 comes from a programme hosted by a comedian, rather than from Orwell, is a measure of the damage done to culture by the very medium that would seek sincerely to dissemi-nate it intact. The problem is that the corresponding commitment to entertain, the more recent need to keep pace with commercial broadcasting companies even if it is not itself seeking to 'increase sales', mutilates and disables the culture that the BBC seeks to promote or preserve. The BBC's treatment of Orwell's concepts on one hand and his critical reputation on the other is symbolic of this dilemma.

We can relate this situation to Orwell's understanding of why and how society is pacified in *1984*. In a passage resonant of Habermas's concerns, the critic Bernard Avishai remarks that 'In Oceania, television degrades private space – first by promis-ing some more compelling public realm, and then by eroding the skills that need privacy and make it worthwhile.'[34] Whilst the BBC may have been founded in the belief that it was offering access to the public realm as another form of its mediation, I'd suggest that there is a striking affinity here between Orwell's imagination of the telescreen in *1984* and the consequences of mass mediation. The compelling public realm, in the BBC's Britain, 2004, is not, of course, that envisaged by Habermas with the same roseate filter as Orwell used to survey 'the English people' – it is *Room 101* and the *Big Brother* house; it is spending Saturday night watching the National Lottery draw.

On the one hand we have the forgetting of history, sponsored by television; on the other hand we have the recollection of history, the transmission of history, also sponsored by television. In June 2003, this took the form of a BBC 2 broadcast, *George Orwell: My Life in Pictures*, a documentary designed to inform a contemporary audience about the writer. This reappraisal of Orwell sought to reclaim the writer from 'a caricature of a tweedy, eccentric and disillusioned rebel' – since Orwell's scepticism towards all forms of power, and most forms of communication, would otherwise render him an unwise role model for the present age. Clearly Orwell's intractability was only one problem; it was compounded by a lack of suitable material for television, as all that Orwell left behind was 'one oil painting and a couple of hundred photographs.' (Presumably the substantial body of writing wasn't much use: someone might have to read it.) Rather than address Orwell's writing and the thought within it, *George Orwell: My Life in Pictures* concentrated on 'Orwell's finest creation…his own artistic and personal reinvention.' As the BBC's press release went on, for this programme 'the pictures are all "invented" – the "archive" has been specially created because there is not a single frame of moving footage of Orwell in existence, nor even one word or one of his trademark hacking coughs on recorded audio.'[35] Whilst this allowed the programme to conform to the currently fashionable trend for dramatized documentaries, the BBC engaged here in exactly the kind of project that in *1984* was Winston Smith's daily occupation at the Ministry of Truth: the fabrication and falsification of history. Though Orwell did not exist on film or recording, in order for him to be understood by today's audiences it is necessary that he should. After all, what do facts matter, or the integrity of a culture? For Chris Durlacher's film 'written essays become authored documentary films shot in the style of the day; events described in diaries are "captured" on home movies; Movietone footage is manipulated to reveal Orwell in the trenches of the Spanish Civil War.'[36]

That the recollection (sic) of history is now likely to be for a tiny audience (in television terms) on a minority channel, rather than – as it was in 1954 – directed towards the whole audience, might be taken as a measure of the decline of public service broadcasting between the 1950s and the present. But we might also see that 'decline' as inevitably bound into the very constitution of broadcasting – its conception that entertainment might somehow occupy the same space as educating and informing about those realities and fostering critical faculties. (This is perhaps because the meaning of the word has changed, with no corresponding shift in its sign, much in the manner of 'doublethink'. There is a slippage from Reith's idea of what constitutes entertainment in the 1920s to what is now the distraction of people from the realities of life; the subjugating of their critical faculties through placeboic distillates.) The one activity suborns the other, or else it pushes it to a sideline – so that it exists primarily for a fraction of that minority that constitutes the managerial class within a democracy. This, of course, is completely at odds with Orwell's hope for the transformation of the English people through plain language about politics and the maintaining of the constant struggle to 'see what is in front of one's nose'.[37] It is also completely at odds with Reith's belief that broadcasting 'teaches concentration.'[38]

Orwell, throughout his writing, even when he is insisting on simplicity and 'commonsense' language in 'Politics and the English Language', nonetheless praises the suppleness and precision of English. 'The greatest quality of English is its enormous range not only of meaning but of *tone*. It is capable of endless subtleties, and of everything from the most high-flown rhetoric to the most brutal coarseness.'[39] But to Orwell this use of language is never for its own sake: literacy and liberty go hand in hand. Commenting on the reduction of language and thought to unthinking habit, he remarks: 'this reduced state of consciousness, if not indispensable, is at any rate favourable to political conformity.'[40] Orwell's belief in keeping a journal is the activity of a historically conscious subject, constantly critiquing its own identity and its place in the world.[41] As Avishai remarks, 'It seemed crucial to Orwell that we write less to say what we think than to discover what we think. We cannot make our thoughts serious or original without steady practice.'[42] Complexity, difficulty, scrutiny: these are essential elements in Orwell's understanding of the subjective capacities of language. But they are anathematic concepts to the commissioning editors of television companies, unless 'scrutiny' is the constant observation offered by the *Big Brother* house in an age when literacy seems designed to promote the reading of advertisements that will make you a good consumer, and the training manuals that may make you a good employee. The BBC, despite its foundation in the Reithian endeavour of intellectually stimulating and transforming the audience, has had to accept the simplification of history, its reduction to 'soundbite' (a good Orwellian 'newspeak' word if ever there was one). Avishai comments that 'freedom as a way of life is of use only to people who...have complex thoughts which they can articulate.'[43] If the hard task of writers, artists and thinkers is to preserve or extend the terrain in which complex language may be used, in which complex thoughts may be held and articulated, it is a task that broadcasters successfully frustrate, even as they proclaim their attempt to extend that same terrain.

With her cast of Room 101, Whiteread, I'd suggest, put this fatal paradox of mass-mediation, as it is articulated in the transmission of Orwell's ideas, into a sculptural form that was, quite literally, 'in front of your nose'. (Given its seemingly incongruous location in the cast court at the V&A there was really little way of avoiding a response to the work.) *Room 101* embodies the processes by which mass-communication in a democratic culture forestalls its own aspirations: Whiteread solidified both a physical emptiness at the heart of Broadcasting House and a moral ambivalence that simultaneously defined and destroyed the BBC's original ethos. *Room 101* stands as a monument to the capacity of broadcasters and writers to tell the truth, even as they simultaneously corrode, belittle and misrepresent the words and concepts which they use to tell it. The cast is at one and the same time a tribute to a heroic but doomed intellectual project and a measurement of the trivialization of culture.

Once again one of Whiteread's artworks metonymized both a present moment (the crisis of the BBC's role, not least in the wake of the Hutton enquiry)[44] and the historical processes through which we had arrived at that point. Nor did it seem as if putting the cast in the V&A, surrounded by the historical residue of British culture, was accidental. For there *Room 101* seemed to be surrounded by forgotten, meaningless objects – the kind of things that commodity culture and frivolous entertainment help us to forget. But these things too were the kind of objects that the BBC was meant to help us remember, to elucidate on our behalf. Weren't they? Or was it that these were indeed the kind of phobic objects, symbols and symptoms of higher culture and the past, of a history written out of existence by the demands of mediation; things that didn't have rights as objects or ideas, unless they could be transformed into image; things ready to be shoved inside 'Room 101' by the next TV personality to appear beside its door?

213

7 Rachel Whiteread, cited by D. Cosper, 'Casting New York: Rachel Whiteread's *Water Tower*', *Metropolis* 17, no. 9 (June 1998), p. 109.

8 In her classic text on Minimalism, Rosalind Krauss develops these issues as a philosophical problem of the relation between illusionism and idealism. See her 'Sense and Sensibility: A Reflection on Post '60s Sculpture', *Artforum*, vol. 12, no. 3 (November 1973), pp. 140–156. For more recent considerations, see H. Foster, 'The Crux of Minimalism', in *The Return of the Real*, pp. 35–69 and J. Meyer, *Minimalism: Art and Polemic in the Sixties* (Yale University Press, 2001).

9 B. Glaser, 'Questions to Stella and Judd', in G. Battcock, (ed.) *Minimal Art: A Critical Anthology* (E.P. Dutton, 1968), p. 158.

10 Fried remarked of literalist objects, 'being distanced by such objects is not, I suggest, entirely unlike being distanced or crowded, by the silent presence of another person: The experience of coming upon literalist objects unexpectedly...can be strongly, if momentarily, disquieting in just this way.' See his 'Art and Objecthood', in *Minimal Art: A Critical Anthology*, p. 128.

11 R. Morris, 'Notes on Sculpture, Part II', in *Minimal Art: A Critical Anthology*, p. 232.

12 M. Merleau-Ponty, *Phenomenology of Perception*, (trans. C. Smith), (Routledge, 2002), p. 239.

13 Ibid, p. 235.

14 Ibid, p. 79.

15 M. Merleau-Ponty, *The Visible and the Invisible*, (trans. A. Lingis), (Northwestern University Press, 1968), p. 134.

16 Ibid, p. 135.

17 Ibid, pp. 263–264.

18 'If Walls Could Talk', p. 56. See also Robert Storr's discussion of the evolution of his response to Whiteread's work in 'Remains of the Day', *Art in America*, vol. 8, no. 4 (April 1999), pp. 105–9, 154.

19 Bruce Nauman in 'Breaking the Silence: An Interview with Bruce Nauman' in J. Kraynak (ed.), *Please Pay Attention Please: Bruce Nauman's Words: Writings and Interviews*, (MIT Press, 2003) p. 324.

20 If Nauman congealed Minimalism's hard, industrial objects into a condition of inertia; Hesse submitted them to the rhythms of obsessional process.

21 As developed in the mid-nineteenth century within the science of thermodynamics by Rudolf Clausius, Ludwig Boltzmann, and Willard Gibbs, who extrapolated from the irreversible flow of heat from hot to cold bodies the existence of an additional property of matter that describes the propensity of closed systems to move towards 'energy drain'; entropy denotes the statistical measure of that tendency towards elemental disorder. Deployed outside its applications within physics, the notion of entropy regained currency from the late 1950s through the 1970s, when it was reshaped by Claude Levi-Strauss along the lines of entropology; fictionalized by Thomas Pynchon in his early story 'Entropy' (1960) and in subsequent novels like *Gravity's Rainbow* (1973), and merged with both art and perceptual psychology in Rudolf Arnheim's account, *Entropy and Art* (1971).

22 R. Smithson, (1966) 'Entropy and the New Monuments', in *Robert Smithson: The Collected Writings*, (University of California Press, 1996) p. 10.

23 Ibid, p. 11.

24 Ibid.

25 Ibid.

26 R. Smithson, (1967) 'A Tour of the Monuments of Passaic, New Jersey', in *Robert Smithson: The Collected Writings*, p. 72.

27 Ibid, p. 73.

28 R. Smithson, (1972) 'The Spiral Jetty', in *Robert Smithson: The Collected Writings*, p. 148.

29 Ibid, p. 149.

30 Ibid, p. 146

31 R. Smithson, (1968), 'A Sedimentation of the Mind: Earth Projects', in *Robert Smithson: The Collected Writings*, p. 104.

32 R. Smithson, (1973), 'Frederick Law Olmsted and the Dialectical Landscape', in *Robert Smithson: The Collected Writings*, p. 160.

33 *Richard Serra: Interviews, etc. 1970–1980* (The Hudson River Museum, 1980), p. 72. For a brilliant analysis of this dialectic, see Y-A. Bois, 'A Picturesque Stroll Around Clara-Clara', *October* 29 (Summer 1984), pp. 32–62.

34 R. Serra, 'Notes from Sight Point Road', *Perspecta*, no. 19 (1982), p. 180.

35 R. Serra and P. Eisenman, 'Interview', *Skyline* (April 1983), p. 16.

36 *Richard Serra: Interviews*, p. 161.

37 Ibid, p. 36.

38 Ibid, pp. 25–28.

39 Bois's 'A Picturesque Stroll' develops the connections of the parallactic turn of Serra's work in relation to mid-eighteenth century architecture (as exemplified by Piranesi's *Carceri*) and landscape gardening (as developed by second generation theoreticians of the picturesque).

40 G. Matta Clark, in an interview with L. Bear, *Avalanche* (December 1974), p. 34.

41 The group included Laurie Anderson, Tina Girouard, Suzanne Harris, Jene Highstein, Bernard Kirschenbaum, Richard Landry, Richard Nonas, Gordon Matta-Clark, and sporadically Jeffrey Lew and Carol Gooden.

42 Bear, *Avalanche*, p. 134.

43 Ibid.

44 G. Matta-Clark, letter reproduced in C. Diserens, (ed.), *Gordon Matta-Clark* (Phaidon Press, 2003), Fig. 199.

45 These concerns also form an implicit horizon for Whiteread's actual intervention into lower Manhattan's skyline. Perhaps to interrupt the intricate connections between structural demolition and expansionist renewal, Whiteread's work assumed the modest and anachronistic form of the *Water Tower*. This work quietly interrupted the city's polymorphous landscape, acting as a reminder of the non-synchronous modes of post-industrial capitalism. The tower's transparent resin body invoked the time of loss — it flickered in and out of existence according to the play of light — and death — installed in June 1998, it vanished from its Grand Street rooftop in June 1999.

46 Interview with Gordon Matta Clark (September 1977), in *Matta-Clark*, (Antwerp, Internationaal Cultureel Centrum, 1978), pp. 9–10.

47 For a rich exploration of Matta-Clark's early building cuts, see P. Lee, 'Improper Objects of Modernity', in *Object To Be Destroyed: The Work of Gordon Matta-Clark* (MIT Press, 2000), pp. 56–112.

48 This exhibition logic owes much to the dialectical relationship between centre and fringe addressed by Smithson's non-sites, which effectively moved art from its place in the museum or gallery to remote and more or less inaccessible locations. 'There's a central focus point which is the non-site,' the artist clarified in an interview, 'the site is the unfocused fringe where your mind loses its boundaries and a sense of the oceanic pervades, as it were.' As we have seen, for Smithson this decentring is also physiological, catapulting the viewer 'towards the outer edge into intractable trajectories that lead to vertigo.' See R. Smithson, (1970) 'Discussions with Heizer, Oppenheim, Smithson' and (1968) 'A Museum of Language in the Vicinity of Art', in *Robert Smithson: The Collected Writings*, p. 249 and p. 94.

49 After scooping out the middle, Matta-Clark, together with a group of artists, bevelled the

cinderblock foundations from the incision point to the back of the house in order to lower the base at that end by a foot. To render the outside space even more porous to the inside, the corners formed by the ceiling and outside walls on the second floor were cut, the sections severed from one side of the house.
50 Robert Smithson, Microfilm 3833, Frame 1176, Archives of American Art.
51 Cited in T. Crow, 'Gordon Matta-Clark', in *Gordon Matta-Clark*, (2003) p. 77.
52 'Alice Aycock interviewed by Joan Simon', in M.J. Jacob, *Gordon Matta-Clark: A Retrospective* (Chicago Museum of Contemporary Art, 1985), p. 33.
53 D. Alberge, 'HOUSE of ghostly memory', *The Independent* (October 26, 1993).
54 R. Krauss, 'Richard Serra/Sculpture', in *Richard Serra: Props* (Wilhelm Lehmbruck Museum, 1994), p. 102.
55 Richard Nonas, 'Gordon's Now, Now', in C. Diserens (ed.) *Gordon Matta-Clark*, (IVAM Centro Julio Gonzalez, 1992), p. 399.
56 For a review of the synagogue's history, see 'Synagogue Closing' in *Jewish Chronicle* (London), August 31, 1984.
57 L.G. Corrin, 'A Conversation with Rachel Whiteread, March 2001' in *Rachel Whiteread* (Serpentine Gallery, 2001).
58 In this work, as in the stair piece, the signs of former occupation are erased by the use of a blank release agent.
59 'If Walls Could Talk', p. 49.
60 Ibid, p. 54.
61 Ibid, p. 49.
62 A. Bazin, 'The Ontology of the Photographic Image', in A. Trachtenberg, (ed.), *Classic Essays on Photography* (Leete's Island Books, 1980), p. 242.
63 See Corrin, 'A Conversation with Rachel Whiteread'.
64 *Camera Lucida*, p. 96.
65 Ibid, p. 93.
66 W. Benjamin, 'A Short History of Photography', in *Classic Essays on Photography*, p. 209.
67 *Aesthetic Theory*, p. 193

GOTHIC PUBLIC ART
AND THE FAILURES OF DEMOCRACY
pp 107 — 127
1 This impression was accentuated by Whiteread's nomination for the Turner Prize in 1991, award of the prize in 1993 and the media hype following the K Foundation's presentation of the artist with a prize for the 'worst' contribution to British art.
2 R. Cork, *Breaking Down the Barriers: Art in the 1990s*, (Yale University Press, 2003) p. 1.
3 Ibid.
4 Defined by Martin Jay as 'that unexpected prick, sting, or cut that [*disturbs*] the intelligibility of the culturally connotated meaning'. M. Jay, *Downcast Eyes: The Denigration of Vision in Twentieth Century French Thought*, (University of California Press, 1994), p. 453.
5 C. Grunenberg, 'Unsolved Mysteries: Gothic Tales from *Frankenstein* to the *Hair-Eating Doll*' in C. Grunenberg, (ed.) *Gothic: Transmutations of Horror in Late Twentieth Century Art*, (MIT Press, 1999) p. 116.
6 F. Jameson, *The Political Unconscious: Narrative as a Socially Symbolic Art*, (Routledge, 1983), p. 34.
7 Ibid.
8 J. A. Walker, *Art and Outrage: Provocation, Controversy and the Visual Arts*, (Pluto Press, 1999), p. 169.
9 Ibid, p. 17.
10 My reference to ideology is here by way of Louis Althusser's formulation in 'Ideology and Ideological State Apparatuses' (in *Essays on Ideology*, (Verso, 1984)) according to which ideology is seen to interpolate subjects and operate on a 'public history' level in the same way as the unconscious does on an 'individual

history' level. For a concise presentation of the evolution of the term see the entry 'Ideology' in M. Payne, (ed.) *A Dictionary of Critical and Cultural Thought*, (Blackwell, 1996).
11 R. Deutsche, *Evictions: Art and Spatial Politics*, (MIT Press, 1996), p. 268.
12 W.J.T. Mitchell, 'Introduction: Utopia and Critique' in W.J.T. Mitchell, (ed.) *Art and the Public Sphere*, (Chicago University Press, 1990), p. 4.
13 This was the title of an edited volume based on a Documenta 11 platform. See O. Enwezor, C. Basualdo, U. Meta Bauer, S. Ghez, S. Maharaj, M. Nash, O. Zaya, (eds.) *Democracy Unrealized, Documenta 11, Platform 1*, (Documenta and Museum Fridericianum and Ostfildern-Ruit/ Hatje Kantz Publishers, 2002).
14 'Introduction: Utopia and Critique' p. 4.
15 In 1993 Whiteread also made a cast of a modernist, more cube-like room, *Untitled (Room)*.
16 See F. Bradley, 'Introduction', *Rachel Whiteread: Shedding Life*, (Tate Publishing, 1996), p. 14. Bradley writes that the artist herself 'has compared the process to the making of a death mask.'
17 M. Cohen, *Profane Illumination: Walter Benjamin and the Paris of Surrealist Revolution*, (California University Press, 1993), p. 133.
18 V. Nabokov, *Lolita* (1995), (Penguin Books, 1989) pp. 162–163.
19 *Warped Space*, p. 148.
20 H. Lefebvre, *The Production of Space*, (1974), (trans. Donald Nicholson-Smith), (Blackwell, 1991)
21 I am paraphrasing Rosalind Krauss's celebrated 'Sculpture in the Expanded Field'. In her discussion of Whiteread's work, Krauss also raises the issue of the surface and writes that the reorganisation of materials 'into a coagulated mass' are separated 'by the "mortiferous layer" of its surface from the living context in which we find it: life/death.' See 'X Marks the Spot', p. 77.
22 See O. Enwezor, 'The Black Box', *Documenta XI, Platform 5: Exhibition Catalogue*, (Documenta and Museum Fridericianum and Ostfildern-Ruit/ Hatje Kantz Publishers, 2002). See also M. Hardt and A. Negri, *Empire*, (Harvard University Press, 2000).
23 Malcolm Miles has elaborated on these issues in his *Art Space and the City: Public Art and Urban Futures*, (Routledge, 1997).
24 In the *Sunday Telegraph* (24 October 1993) John McEwen remarks 'so it's a political statement?' and Whiteread replies: 'In part, yeah, but I hope this will be obvious from the piece. I'm not going to stand on the street corner saying: 'This is a political statement.' It's just a typical Victorian house most people in England have lived in at some time or other. And the context is important. It's site-specific and outside. I chose the location very carefully. Just about everything is there.'
25 D. Harvey, *Spaces of Hope*, (University of California Press, 2000), p. 183.
26 Ibid.
27 See F. Jameson, *Postmodernism, or the Cultural Logic of Late Capitalism*, (Verso 1991), p. 67 and pp. 172–175. The phrase appears as the heading of a chapter on video but acquires its full meaning in the chapter on painting in connection with the death of the subject, either individual or collective. Jameson elaborates: 'Chagall's folk iconography without Judaism or the peasants, Klee's stick drawings without his peculiar personal project, schizophrenic art without schizophrenia, 'surrealism' without its manifesto or its avant-garde'. pp. 174–175.

AS THE WEATHER
pp 128 — 148
1 'Looking Up' is what Whiteread would entreat the viewer to do: to take account of the fabric of the urban

217

surroundings by looking up at the skyline as well as down at the street. See L. Neri, (ed.), *Looking Up: Rachel Whiteread's Water Tower*, (The Public Art Fund, 1999).
2 The details behind this back-history are largely drawn from T. Eccles, 'Vanishing Point: The Making of Water Tower', in *Looking Up*, pp. 21–29.
3 Hirst organized the show in 1988, including his peers from Goldsmiths College. For a useful introduction to the topic see G. Williams, 'Pause...Rewind...Press Play. Reviewing British Art in the 1990s', in *Art from the UK* (Sammlung Goetz, 1998), pp. 15–21.
4 On the thematics of the uncanny (as an oppressive memory trace) in *House*, see *Warped Space*, pp. 143–149. Also see D. Massey, 'Space-Time and the Politics of Location', *Architectural Design*, vol. 68, no. 3/4 (March–April 1998), pp. 34–37.
5 C. Vogel, 'SoHo Site Specific: On the Roof', *New York Times*, June 11, 1998, Arts and Leisure, p. 4.
6 'Vanishing Point', p. 24. The cost of the sculpture was $270,000 USD.
7 B. Columina, 'I Dreamt I Was a Wall', in *Rachel Whiteread: Transient Spaces*, p. 72.
8 L. Sante, 'Cabin in the Sky', in *Looking Up*, p. 89
9 Bernd and Hilla Becher quoted in 'Vanishing Point', p. 26. Also see B. & H. Becher, *Water Towers* (MIT Press, 1988).
10 'Cabin in the Sky', p. 89.
11 For an expanded history of the area in relationship to contemporary art, see my *Object to Be Destroyed*.
12 Among other books that take up the history of lower Manhattan in the sixties and seventies – and Robert Moses's impact on it – see R. Fitch, *The Assassination of New York* (Verso, 1993).
13 Trisha Brown quoted in *Looking Up*, p. 171.
14 P. Span, 'Chelsea Morning: a Part of New York Awakens', *Washington Post*, January 7, 1997, p. E3
15 R. Storr, 'Remains of the Day', *Art in America*, Vol. 87, No. 4 (April 1999), p. 154.
16 R. Smith, 'The Ghosts of SoHo', *New York Times*, August 28, 1998, pp. E1–2.
17 C. Berwick, 'Western Expansion', *Artnews*, Vol. 101, no. 4, (April 2002) p. 110. Also see B. Pollack, 'Westward, Ho!' *Artnews*, Vol. 97, no. 5 (May 1998) pp. 132–137.
18 S. Douglas, 'The Real Estate Market for Galleries: Chelsea Ever More Expensive', *Art Newspaper*, no. 114, (May 2001) p. 56.
19 R. Pogrebin, 'Report Says Artists' Arrival Can Push out Neighbors', *New York Times*, The Arts, November 11, 2002, pp. E1 and E4.
20 'Vanishing Point', p. 26.
21 J. Hall, 'East Meets West', *Artforum*, Vol. 38, no. 8 (April 2000) p. 49.

THE SHIMMER OF INDUSTRIAL FORM
pp 149 – 161
1 R. Barthes, *La Chambre clair* (Éditions du Seuil, 1980) Translated as *Camera Lucida*, p. 93. Here is one art historian's account of the original statement of this argument: 'In Bergson's philosophy, every expressive medium, whether it be plastic, literary or musical, is the end of a process whereby the inner, manifold self becomes spatialized through the process of self-representation. Psychologically, such externalization is manifest in the transition from a highly emotive and alogical state to a non-emotive, rational state of mind. The temporal analogue for this change is the transposition of indivisible duration into a multiplicity of moments each external to the next, whose divisible state veils their inner interpenetration. This fragmented self is both rational and adapted to social life. Thus it becomes evident that all forms of self-representation would seem self-defeating—

inevitably the profound self is refracted and impoverished through the very mechanism of self-representation. Nonetheless, there are degrees of spatialization within these modes of self-representation. (...) Bergson regarded all forms of representation as distorted refractions of a profound, ineffable self.' (M. Antliff, *Inventing Bergson: cultural politics and the Parisian avant-garde*, (Princeton University Press, 1993), p. 48.
2 'A House is not a Home', p. 38.
3 See H. Lehen, *Cool Conduct: The Culture of Distance in Weimar Germany* (University of California Press, 2002), pp. ix, xi.
4 'If Walls Could Talk', p. 52.
5 See, for example, Victor Burgin's review in *Creative Camera* no. 215 (November 1982) pp. 730–730 among others.
6 *Camera Lucida*, p. 98.
7 D. J. Boorstin, *The Image; or, What Happened to the American Dream* (Atheneum Press, 1962), pp. 257–258.
8 J. Baudrillard, from *The System of Objects*, reprinted in M. Poster, (ed.), *Jean Baudrillard: Selected Writings*, (Stanford University Press, 1988), p. 11.
9 Barthes 'ça a été'. *Camera Lucida*, p. 100.
10 Ibid, p. 98.
11 G.W.F. Hegel, *The Phenomenology of Spirit*, (trans. A.V. Miller), (Oxford University Press, 1979), p. 476.
12 'Notes on the Index, Part I', p. 203. 'Barthes has already written the outlines of a critical text on Whiteread's art, in his own consideration of photography as a kind of traumatic death mask which is paradoxically both "structured"...and "asymbolic".' (R. Krauss, 'X Marks the Spot', p. 76.)
13 Rachel Whiteread, *The Times*, 12 January 1994
14 New Statesman, 20 September, 1996, p. 41.
15 'A House is not a Home', p. 32.
16 A. Vidler, 'A Dark Space', in *Rachel Whiteread: House* (Phaidon, 1995), p. 72.
17 Whiteread quoted in Lynn Barber, 'Some day, my plinth will come', *The Observer*, May 27, 2001. This in itself is a somewhat bizarre claim, given the almost complete abrogation of historical relevance attributed to most YBAs by critics such as Julian Stallabrass.
18 J. Habermas, *The Structural Transformation of the Public Sphere: An Inquiry into a Category of Bourgeois Society* (MIT Press, 1991); F. Jameson, 'The Vanishing Mediator; or, Max Weber as Storyteller', *New German Critique* (Winter 1973), 1: 52–89; E. Balibar, 'Europe: Vanishing Mediator', *Constellations* 10:3 (2003), pp. 312–338.
19 'Some day, my plinth will come'.
20 S. Jenkins, 'Art house in a cul-de-sac', *The Spectator*, 21 November 1993.
21 'Introduction', *Rachel Whiteread: Shedding Life*, p. 11.
22 *Phenomenology of Spirit*, p. 476.

RACHEL WHITEREAD'S
JUDENPLATZ MEMORIAL IN VIENNA
pp 162 – 172
1 This essay is adapted from my *At Memory's Edge: After-images of the Holocaust in Contemporary Art and Architecture* (Yale University Press, 2000). In it, I expand on themes I first explored in 'The Counter-monument: Memory against Itself in Germany Today', *Critical Inquiry* 18 (Winter 1992) pp. 267–296. Also see my *The Texture of Memory: Holocaust Memorials and Meaning* (Yale University Press, 1993), pp. 27–48.
2 For a record of this competition, see *Denkmal fur die ermordeten Juden Europas: Kurzdokumentation* (Senatsverwaltung fur Bau und Wohnungswesen, 1995). For a collection of essays arguing against building this monument, see *Der Wettbewerb fur das 'Denkmal fur die ermordeten Juden Europas': Eine*

Streitschrift (Verlag der Kunst/Neue Gesellschaft fur Bildende Kunst, 1995). On the proposal to blow up the *Brandenburger Tor*, see H. Hoheisel, 'Aschrottbrunnen - Denk-Stein-Sammlung - Brandenburger Tor - Buchenwald. Vier Erinnerungsversuche,' in N. Berg, J. Jochimsen, & B. Stiegler, (eds.), *Shoah - Formen der Erinnerung: Geschichte, Philosophie, Literatur, Kunst* (Wilhelm Fink Verlag, 1996), pp. 253–266.
3 See A. Fischer & M. Glameier, (eds.), *The Missing House* (Berliner Kunstlerprogram des DAAD fur das Heimatmuseum Berlin-Mitte, 1990).
4 'Introduction', *Shedding Life*, p. 8.
5 *Judenplatz Wien 1996: Wettbewerb Mahnmal und Gedenkstatte fur die judischen Opfer des Naziregimes in Osterreich 1938-1945* (Stadt Wien/Kunsthalle Wien, 1996), p. 94.
6 Storr, p. 109
7 'The Uncanny', p. 241.
8 *Aesthetic Theory*, p. 262
9 'The Uncanny', p. 241.

LESSONS FROM WHAT'S POOR
pp 173 – 196

1 Following the removal of *Monument* a carpet of spikes was installed on top of the plinth.
2 Barry's original fountains now stand outside the Parliament Building in Ottawa, Canada.
3 'Space, Knowledge, and Power' p. 351.
4 Railton's monument was vigorously contested in Parliamentary committee because of its impact on Nash's planned sight lines for the National Gallery.
5 *Passages in Modern Sculpture*, p.10
6 S. Freud, 'A Note Upon the Mystic Writing Pad' (1925 [1924]), in J. Strachey, (ed. & trans.) *The Standard Edition of the Complete Psychological Works of Sigmund Freud, Vol. XIX*, (Hogarth Press, 1961), pp. 227–234.
7 See for example W. Brock, *A Biographical Sketch of Sir Henry Havelock*, (James Nisbet & Co, 1858) and L. Taylor, *The Story of Sir Henry Havelock, the Hero of Lucknow*, (Nelson, 1894). The latter, in a series entitled 'Stories of Noble Lives', concludes that for a man 'faithful to his country because faithful to his God,' 'the path of duty was the way to glory.'
8 For example W. Maccall's pamphlet *The Career and Character of Charles James Napier, the Conqueror of Scinde*, (Truelove, 1857) makes no mention of any memorial scheme or monument, and establishes a discourse around its subject as both a loyal servant and a figure largely excluded from reward by the establishment. Maccall also remarks that Napier largely sympathized with the political aspirations of the Chartists.
9 'Some day my plinth will come'.
10 Those statues that have to a large degree conformed to earlier tradition have often been the ones most obviously defaced by protestors – whether Churchill's, endowed with a turf mohican by May-Day marchers, or that of Lord Harris, chief of Bomber Command in World War 2 and the man charged as responsible for the strategic targeting of German civilian areas rather than military or industrial targets.
11 J. Derrida, '*Point de folie – maintenant l'Architecture*' in *Bernard Tschumi – La case vide – La Villette 1985*, (Architectural Association, 1986), p. 5.
12 Assembled from solid granite blocks, the plinth has a minimal interior volume. In fact, because the plinth itself is a listed monument, the mould for *Monument* was not taken directly from it, but from a specially made replica.
13 The full material description of *Monument*, as installed in Trafalgar Square, is 'Resin and granite'. See *Rachel Whitehead* (Haunch of Venison, 2002), p.27.
14 *Passages in Modern Sculpture*, p.10.
15 *Ibid* p.18.
16 *Ibid*.

17 'Rachel Whiteread interviewed by Andrea Rose', p.32. B. Colomina in *Rachel Whiteread: Transient Spaces*, p. 86, misattributes this remark to a discussion of *Water Tower*. Whiteread and Rose are in fact discussing the resin floor-piece *Corridor* installed in the British Pavilion at the 1997 Venice Biennale.
18 *Passages in Modern Sculpture*, pp. 20–21.
19 In this respect, for *Monument* at least, though clearly not for a project like *House*, I would disagree with Krauss's perception of Whiteread's work as ultimately working within 'the domain of the entropic', but rather suggest that *Monument* acts as a blocking of time that introduces a self-cancelling cycle. (See 'X Marks the Spot', pp. 75–76) Rather than accepting the transcendent temporality of the monument or the entropic motion of the anti-forms of post-minimalism, *Monument* sets the monumental tradition in aspic, as it were.
20 'Of Other Spaces' p. 24.
21 N. Foote, 'The Apotheosis of the Crummy Space', *Artforum*, (October 1976).
22 A work that is, of course, doubly cast – first thrown matter, then mould of the juncture between wall and floor; a work that is, like *Monument*, continued in a reversal and displacement of the cast space; a work that is, to a degree, like *Monument* in its ephemerality. But where *Casting*'s temporary status is one of material condition – Serra melts the work down – *Monument*'s is a condition of location. Ultimately the piece, together with replica granite plinth though not a replica Trafalgar Square, nor replica historical tradition, will be installed in a permanent collection.
23 *Passages in Modern Sculpture*, p. 57. Krauss is commenting here on Gabo, but as she goes on to show despite one's apparent critique of the other, both ultimately work towards a notion of transcendent reality.
24 *Ibid*, p. 53.
25 *Ibid*.
26 *Ibid*, p. 57.
27 *Ibid*, p. 58.
28 *Ibid*, pp. 60–61.
29 *Ibid*, p. 55.
30 J. Lacan, 'The Agency of the letter in the unconscious or reason since Freud' in *Écrits: A Selection*, (A. Sheridan, trans.) (Routledge, 1977), p. 153. See also J-L. Nancy, & P. Lacoue-Labarthe, *The Title of the Letter: A Reading of Lacan* (State University of New York Press: 1992) p. 52.
31 P. Elliott, 'Sculpting Nothing: An Introduction to the Work of Rachel Whiteread' in *Rachel Whiteread* (National Galleries of Scotland, 2001) p. 9.

LIVE AS IF SOMEONE IS ALWAYS WATCHING YOU
pp 197 – 213

This essay is dedicated to Michael Haynes-Smallbone, who encouraged a thirteen-year old working class boy in a very snobbish grammar school to read first *The Road to Wigan Pier*, then Orwell's *Collected Essays and Journalism*. He also taught me the value of dissent.
1 *Room 101* was commissioned as part of the Broadcasting House Public Art Programme, 2002–2008, a project drawing 'inspiration from the BBC's role and remit in the 21st century.' (*www.publicartonline.org.uk/news/reports/bbc_broadcasting_house.html*). The project as a whole is curated and managed by Modus Operandi Art Consultants. Orwell's office also features at the end of a film by Tom Gidley, made as part of the same project.
2 J.C.W. Reith, *Broadcast over Britain* (Hodder and Stoughton, 1924). See pp. 147–154 and p. 219.
3 *Ibid*, p. 18.
4 Orwell was working for the Indian service at a time when the Axis powers were trying to foster Indian nationalism as a force against the British, when some Indian nationalists were trying to recruit forces to fight

alongside the Japanese army in Burma, and the Japanese were making limited bombing raids on India.

5 G. Orwell, *1984*, (Penguin Books, 2000), p. 162.

6 G. Orwell, (1946) 'James Burnham and the Managerial Revolution' in *Collected Essays, Journalism and Letters of George Orwell, Vol. 4, 'In Front of Your Nose'*, *1945–1950* (Penguin Books, 1970), pp. 192–215. Parts of Burnham's writing are uncannily reflected in Emmanuel Goldstein's *Theory and Practice of Oligarchical Socialism*, the book used by the Party to trap the dissident Winston and Julia in *1984*.

7 'James Burnham', pp. 205–207. Orwell rightly critiques Burnham for his admiration of Nazi Germany and the USSR as managerially efficient societies. But Burnham's ideas are, at the level of politics, neutral, since they constitute a meta-ideology which can absorb any regime, from the free-market to the centralised economy, in the name of efficiency and the perpetuation of an oligarchical management class (access to which is granted itself not by birth-right but 'merit').

8 I'd suggest that with the valorisation of the manager as index of social 'progress', those older roles, if pursued at all, become 'brandings' of the self, by which one is known and marketed in the public sphere. Baudelaire recognised this early on as a condition of 'modern' society. For a contemporary rethinking of the process see U. Lehmann, 'The Trademark Tracey Emin' in M. Merck & C. Townsend (eds.), *The Art of Tracey Emin* (Thames & Hudson, 2002). Warhol might be understood as partially transcending this situation by becoming his own brand manager, in the sense that he employs others to endlessly reproduce 'him'.

9 *1984*, p. 72, p. 75.

10 Ibid, p. 74.

11 Ibid, p. 46.

12 Ibid, p. 89.

13 A. Briggs, *The History of Broadcasting in the United Kingdom, Vol. IV, Sound and Vision*, (Oxford University Press, 1995) p. 166.

14 A. Briggs, *The History of Broadcasting in the United Kingdom, Vol. I, The Birth of Broadcasting*, (Oxford University Press, 1995) p. 17.

15 Ibid.

16 B.P. Emmett, 'The Television Audience in the United Kingdom' *Journal of the Royal Statistical Society* (1956) p. 284, cited in *History of Broadcasting in the United Kingdom, Vol. IV*, p. 11.

17 *History of Broadcasting in the United Kingdom, Vol. I*, p. 16; see the table reproduced from Emmett in *History of Broadcasting in the United Kingdom, Vol. IV*, p. 11, for the rapid change in class distribution of the TV audience between 1947 and 1954.

18 *The History of Broadcasting in the United Kingdom, Vol. IV*, p. 161.

19 'Ideology and Ideological State Apparatuses', *passim*.

20 *1984*, p. 198. Goldstein's book is the work of party functionaries, produced to entrap potential dissidents.

21 G. Beauchamp, 'Big Brother in America', *Social Theory and Practice*, Vol. 10, No. 3, (Fall 1984) p. 249.

22 *1984*, p. 296.

23 Cited on *www.24hourmuseum.org.uk/nwh_gfx_en/ART18662.html*

24 *1984*, p. 296.

25 M. Tracey, *The Decline and Fall of Public Service Broadcasting*, (Oxford University Press, 1998) p. 20.

26 'Channel 4 looks to Big Time Big Brother', *The Guardian*, 3 May, 2002.

27 *1984*, p. 3

28 Ibid.

29 Ibid, p. 272.

30 BBC press release, 29 July, 2002.

31 G. Orwell, 'The English People' in *Collected Essays,*

Journalism and Letters of George Orwell, Vol. 3, 'As I Please', 1943–1945, (Penguin Books, 1970), p. 26.

32 See *History of Broadcasting in the United Kingdom, Vol. IV*, p. 628, n. 6. I'm indebted to my colleague Cathy Johnson for her advice on the anecdotal nature of audience research in the 1950s. Briggs's claims for the audience for the 1954 production should be treated with a degree of scepticism.

33 *The Structural Transformation of the Public Sphere*, p. 165.

34 B. Avishai, 'Orwell and the English Language', in I. Howe (ed.) *1984 Revisited: Totalitarianism in Our Century*, (Harper & Row, 1983) pp. 67–68.

35 All quotes from *www.bbc.co.uk/pressoffice/pressreleases/stories/2003/04_april/29/george_orwell.shtml* The 'trademark cough' [part of Orwell's self-promotion as brand if you give credence to his 'artistic and personal reinvention'] was because the writer was slowly dying from tuberculosis.

36 Ibid. I'd like to think there was a degree of irony implicit in the decision to make the programme this way – but I'm not that optimistic.

37 G. Orwell, 'In Front of Your Nose' in *Collected Essays, Journalism and Letters of George Orwell, Vol. 4*, p. 154.

38 *Broadcast Over Britain*, p. 187.

39 'The English People', p. 41.

40 'Politics and the English Language', in *Collected Essays, Journalism and Letters of George Orwell, Vol. 4*, pp. 165–166.

41 'In Front of Your Nose', p. 154.

42 'Orwell and the English Language', p. 63.

43 Ibid.

44 During the Iraq war of 2003, BBC Radio 4 broadcast a report by one of its journalists, Andrew Gilligan, which alleged that the government had 'sexed up' (that is, unreasonably glossed or biased) a dossier of information gathered by state security agencies in order to present a more favourable case for an unpopular military action to both Parliament and public. A high-ranking civil servant, Dr. David Kelly, who - as an expert on the 'weapons of mass destruction' that the government claimed Iraq possessed and could readily deploy - would have been privy to debates about the dossier's contents, was identified as the source of the information in Gilligan's report. Dr. Kelly was soon after found dead near his home. An inquiry under the aegis of Lord Hutton was commissioned by the government, scrutinizing aspects of the BBC's reporting and the Ministry of Defence's handling both of information and its wayward official. Hutton's report largely exonerated all government agencies, whilst its findings against the BBC led to the resignation of the Chairman of its Board of Governors, its Director-General, Gregg Dyke, and the especially vilified Gilligan. Despite this report there remained a pervasive sense that what became known in 'newspeak' (or 'news-speak') as 'the dodgy dossier' *had* misrepresented the case for military action. (Nearly a year after the war none of the claimed 'weapons of mass destruction' had been found.) An adequate rehearsal of all aspects of the subsequent (and continuing) battle between the BBC and the government of Prime Minister Blair would occupy more space than this essay allows. Such an overview requires the scope of a book and historical perspective. It may also require access to documents that are, due to 'state security', never likely to be made available to researchers. Alternatively, it might require the condensation of, simultaneously, a present crisis and its historical roots in the state sanctioning of the BBC, and the more general, but crucial, question of language and power. It might, then, require an artwork such as *Room 101*.

LIST OF ILLUSTRATIONS AND CREDITS

1 *Untitled (Collected Works)* (1998), plaster, polystyrene and steel. Photo: d'Offay Gallery
2 *Closet* (1988), plaster, felt and wood. Photo: d'Offay Gallery
3 *Untitled (Black Bed)* (1991), fibreglass and rubber. Photo: d'Offay Gallery
4 *Untitled* (1987), sellotape and air. Photo: Gagosian Gallery
5 *Untitled (Six Spaces)* (1994), resin, 6 units. Photo: d'Offay Gallery
6 *Untitled (25 Spaces)* (1995), resin, 25 units. Photo: d'Offay Gallery. Photo credit British Council
7 *Untitled (Floor)* (1994–95), resin. Photo: d'Offay Gallery
8 *Untitled (One Hundred Spaces)* (1995), resin, 100 units. Photo: d'Offay Gallery
9 *Untitled (Air Bed II)* (1992), rubber and neoprene. Photo: d'Offay Gallery. Photo credit Volker Nauman
10 *Untitled (Book Corridors)* (1997–98), plaster, polystyrene, steel and wood. Photo: d'Offay Gallery
11 *Untitled (Yellow Bed, Two Parts)* (1991), dental plaster. Photo: d'Offay Gallery. Photo credit Ed Woodman Two Parts
12 *Table and Chair (Clear)* (1994), rubber. Photo: d'Offay Gallery
13 *Untitled (Room)* (1993), plaster. Photo: d'Offay Gallery. Photo credit Tate Gallery Photography Department Two Variants
14 *Valley* (1990), plaster and glass. Photo: d'Offay Gallery. Photo credit Ed Woodman.
15 *Ether* (1990), plaster. Photo: d'Offay Gallery. Photo credit Ed Woodman
16 *Untitled (Clear Slab)* (1992), rubber. Photo: d'Offay Gallery
17 *Untitled (Wardrobe)* (1994), plaster and glass. Photo: d'Offay Gallery
18 *Ghost* (1990), plaster on steel frame. Photo: d'Offay Gallery. Saatchi Collection
19 *Mantle* (1988), plaster and glass. Photo: d'Offay Gallery
20 *Yellow Leaf* (1989), plaster, formica and wood. Photo: d'Offay Gallery. Collection Gulbenkian Foundation, Lisbon
21 *Untitled (Amber Double Bed)* (1991), rubber and high density foam. Photo: d'Offay Gallery. Photo credit Alex Hartley
22 *Untitled (Amber Bed)* (1991), rubber. Photo: d'Offay Gallery. Photo credit Alex Hartley Two Variants
23 *Light Switches* (1996–98), two R-type photographs. Photo: Luhring Augustine Gallery
24 Detail of *Untitled (Room)*. Photo: Mathias Schormann.
25 *Model of Untitled (Wall)* (1999), mixed media. Photo: Luhring Augustine Gallery
26 *Untitled (Pulp)* (1999), plaster, polystyrene and steel in 5 section. Photo: d'Offay Gallery

27 *Ghost* (1990), plaster on steel frame. Photo: d'Offay Gallery. Saatchi Collection
28 *Demolished* (1996), 4 of 12 duotone screenprints. Photo: d'Offay Gallery
29 *Untitled (Stairs)* (2001), mixed media. Photo: d'Offay Gallery
30 *Untitled (Basement)* (2001), mixed media. Photo: d'Offay Gallery. Photo credit Ellen Labenski
31 *Untitled (Cast Iron Floor)* (2001), cast iron and black patina. Photo: d'Offay Gallery
32 *Untitled (Apartment)* (2000–01), plasticised plaster, wood and steel. Photo: d'Offay Gallery. Photo credit Ellen Labenski
33 *Untitled (House)* (1993). Photo: d'Offay Gallery. Photo credit Sue Ormerod Three Variants
34 *Study for 'House'* (1992–93), correction fluid on laser copy. Photo: d'Offay Gallery
35 *House* (1993). Photo: d'Offay Gallery. Photo credit Sue Ormerod
36 *House* (1993). Photo: d'Offay Gallery. Photo credit Sue Ormerod
37 Photograph taken during the making of *House* (Autumn 1993). Photo: d'Offay Gallery
38 *Water Tower* (1998), resin cast of the interior of a wooden water tank. Photo: d'Offay Gallery. Photo credit Marian Harders
39 *Water Tower Project* (1998), acrylic varnish on screenprint. Photo: Luhring Augustine Gallery
40 Trisha Brown, *Roof Piece* (1974). Photo: Babette Mangolte.
41 *Water Tower* (June 1998–June 1999), resin cast of the interior of a water tank. Photo: d'Offay Gallery. Photo Credit Marian Harders
42 *Holocaust Memorial* (1995). Photo: d'Offay Gallery. Photo credit Werner Kaligofsky
43 Maquette for *Holocaust Memorial* (1995), mixed media. Photo: d'Offay Gallery. Photo credit Mike Bruce
44 *Holocaust Memorial* (1995). Photo: d'Offay Gallery. Photo credit Werner Kaligofsky
45 *Monument* (2001), resin and granite. Photo: Luhring Augustine Gallery
46 William Behnes, *Sir Henry Havelock* (1861), bronze statue. Photo: Jo Broughton.
47 *Untitled (Rubber Plinth)* (1996), rubber and polystyrene. Photo: d'Offay Gallery
48 *Untitled (Elongated Plinths)* (1998), plastic and urethane foam (three elements each). Photo: d'Offay Gallery. Photo credit Mike Bruce
49 *Monument* (2001), resin and granite. Photo: Luhring Augustine Gallery
50 Umberto Boccioni, *Development of a Bottle in Space* (1912), bronze.
51 *Untitled (Room 101)*, (2003), mixed media. Photo: Gagosian Gallery

NOTES ON CONTRIBUTORS

ANGELA DIMITRAKAKI is Lecturer in Art History at the University of Southampton. Her research and publications focus on the intersection of feminist politics, geography and contemporary art. She is co-editor of *Private Views: Spaces and Gender in Contemporary Art from Britain and Estonia* (2000), *Independent Practices: Representation, Location and History in Contemporary Visual Art* (2000) and *ReFrame: Dialogues on Contemporary Art and Culture* (2002). She is currently working on women artists' film andvideo in Europe.

JENNIFER R. GROSS is Seymour H. Knox, Jr. Curator of Modern and Contemporary Art at the Yale University Art Gallery and visiting critic at the Yale School of Art. Recent exhibition projects include 'Edgar Degas: Defining the Modernist Edge', 'Between Language and Form' and 'The Colossal Keepsake Corporation and Claes Oldenburg's Lipstick'. She is currently working on a travelling exhibition of the Société Anonyme Collection and establishing the Robert and Evelyn Doran Artist-In-Residence Program at Yale University Art Gallery.

SHELLEY HORNSTEIN is Professor of Art and Architectural History at York University, Toronto, Canada and has published widely on the examination of concepts of place and spatial politics in architectural and urban sites. She is editor of *Capital Culture: A Reader on Modernist Legacies, State Institutions, and the Value(s) of Art* (2000), *Image and Remembrance: Representation and The Holocaust* (2002), and *Impossible Images: Contemporary Art after the Holocaust* (2003). Her current project is a book entitled *Losing Site: The Resonance of Architecture and Place.*

SUSAN LAWSON is an independent writer based in London, and an editor in the field of contemporary art. With a background in architecture and visual theory, she has previously published on the work of Cornelia Parker in the journal *n.paradoxa.*

PAMELA M. LEE is Associate Professor of Art History at Stanford University. She is the author of *Object to be Destroyed: The Work of Gordon Matta-Clark* (2000) and *Chronophobia: On Time in the Art of the 1960* (2004) and a regular contributor to *Artforum.* Her writings have also appeared in *October, Texte zur Kunst* and *Parkett.*

MELANIE MARIÑO is Assistant Professor of Contemporary Art at the University of Wisconsin-Milwaukee. Recent publications include 'Disposable Matter' for the Walker Art Center exhibition catalogue, *The Last Picture Show: Artists Using Photography, 1960 –1982*, and 'Almost Not Photography' for *Conceptual Art: Theory, Myth, and Practice* (2004). She is preparing a book on conceptual photography.

BLAKE STIMSON teaches for the Art History and Critical Theory programs at the University of California, Davis. Recent publications include 'I am the Social' (Artforum, November 2003) and, co-edited with Gregory Sholette, *Collectivism After Modernism* (forthcoming).

CHRIS TOWNSEND is Lecturer in the Department of Media Arts, Royal Holloway, University of London. Amongst other monographs he is the author of *A World at Random: The Art of Boyle Family, (*forthcoming 2004*)* and the editor of a number of volumes on contemporary artists, including *The Art of Tracey Emin,* (with Mandy Merck) and *The Art of Bill Viola.* He is currently working on a book about post-YBA art in London and a variety of site-specific projects with young artists.

JAMES E. YOUNG is Professor and Chair of Judaic and Near Eastern Studies at the University of Massachusetts Amherst. He is the author of *At Memory's Edge* (2000), The Texture of Memory (1993), *Writing and Rewriting the Holocaust* (1988), and editor of *The Art of Memory* (1994).

ACKNOWLEDGMENTS

Thanks goes to Rachel Whiteread and her assistant Hazel Willis – to whom we owe particular gratitude; to Pernilla Holmes, Graham Southern and Harry Blain at Haunch of Venison; to Anthony d'Offay and James Elliot at Anthony d'Offay Gallery; to Claudia Altman-Siegel and Nathalie Afnan at Luhring Augustine Gallery; to Cristina Colomar at Gagosian Gallery. Chris Townsend would like to thank Sophie Symons for invaluable conversations concerning *Monument* and Foucault's critique of institutional power, and looks forward to many more.

INDEX